D1 DREAM

RECRUITING INSIGHTS FROM 60 DIVISION 1 ATHLETES

Accounts of Life as a D1 Athlete... *"in their words"*

Marita Decker and Caroline Zadina

Direct commentary regarding specific athletic experiences are the opinions of the athletes' interviewed, and do not reflect the opinions of the authors or Publisher.

No responsibility is assumed by the authors or Publisher for any injury and/or damage to persons or property from use of methods, instructions, or ideas contained in this material. No suggested method or activity should be carried out unless, in the reader's judgment, it is appropriate and justified.

All rights reserved. Printed in the United States of America. Except as permitted under the United States Copyright Act of 1976, no part of this publication may be reproduced or distributed in any form, or by any means, or stored in a database or retrieval system, without the prior written permission of the authors.

Cover Image: Evgenii Matrosov/ Shutterstock.com

Copyright 2017 © FutureCourse Education, Publishing

ISBN: 978-0692965221

To my three children, and their many teammates...
Who showed me the determination, strength, and tolerance of committed athletes.
Thank you for living with courage and conviction.

Thank you to Gabrielle Zadina, Soccer, University of Cincinnati and Case Western Reserve University, and Bianca Perry, Soccer, DePaul University, for athlete recruitment and interviewing support.

Thank you to Tayler Fitts, Soccer, University of Cincinnati and Indiana University, for cover insight and design.

Contents

Preface   7
   From a former college athlete, to a future college athlete
   From an athlete's parent, to an athlete's parent
   Our views on college recruiting today

Introduction   13

How to Best Use This Book   15

Chapter 1: Congratulations! And, This is Hard   17
   Athlete Insights: the differences between high school and college athletics

Chapter 2: Begin With the End in Mind   25
   Athlete Insights: the best of times and lessons learned

Chapter 3: Find Your Winning Context   43
   Athlete Insights: coaches, team dynamics, and the social life of D1 athletes

Chapter 4: Know the Risks   69
   Athlete Insights: the worst of times for these D1 athletes

Chapter 5: Prepare for Academic Practicalities   83
   Athlete Insights: academics, professors and career prep

Chapter 6: Plan for Common Challenges   99
   Athlete Insights: handling the tough times- injuries, homesickness, travel, etc.

Chapter 7: Informed Recruiting-Finding a Great Match   111
   Athlete Insights: parent to parent, and athlete to athlete

Appendices   125
   1. **Athletic Programs and Sports Reflected in this Version**
   2. **The Research Protocol for the Book**
   3. **Your Input Wanted**
      Please let us know about your experiences during recruiting or as an athlete. We value your input and would look forward to including it in our next update. As with the current book, all submissions are treated with the utmost confidentiality and will remain anonymous. Email us at: d1dream.info@gmail.com.

Preface

This book is by Division 1 athletes, for high school athletes and their families, as they navigate the college athletic recruiting process. It is written with both the athlete and parent in mind as we, my daughter and I, have composed this book together with joint insight, balancing the athlete and parent perspective of college athletic recruiting. While first and foremost directed to high school athletes embarking on their recruiting journey, we hope that parents also take time to fully engage in this exciting and challenging process. Like the familiar saying goes, "two minds are greater than one," our hope is that athlete-parent teams work together to provide checks and balances throughout the recruiting process, to ensure clear thinking and thoughtful critique of all potential college options. Ultimately, the goal is for you, as the reader, whether athlete or parent, to gain insight and perspective of life as a college athlete at the Division 1 (D1) level. We selected to focus solely on D1 athletics because its brand and competitive arena seem to entice high school athletes looking to continue in their sport at the college level. So, whether you are an athlete, a parent, college counselor or athletic advisor, this book is meant for you. It is comprised of real life stories of D1 athletes, so that you may learn from their experiences, and use this knowledge to guide a fully informed athletic and academic college decision.

From a former college athlete, to a future college athlete

Go get 'em!

As a retired college athlete looking back on my own recruiting process, I hope that this book helps you as you search for your right college match. I encourage you to look beyond the 'brand,' and beyond the facilities and perks. College sport is not easy, and the only way to ensure success is to start prepared. While it may seem like recruitment is the biggest hurdle, at least that's what I thought, I assure you that it is by far the easiest part of being a college athlete. I urge you to take this process seriously, and really consider your options wisely and fully. Think long and hard about what makes you happy, what you like to do beyond sport, and who you want to be when you graduate in four years. I hope that you read these stories, and from them, gain a sense of encouragement and confidence that you are one step closer, on feet more ready and sure, to decide on a college that is right for you as a whole person: academically, socially, athletically.

Remember, *to play your best, you must be at your best, and only those who know THEIR best, are ready to succeed.*

From an athlete's parent, to an athlete's parent

"If only I knew then, what I know now ..."

I have three dedicated athletes, two who recruited early in high school to coveted D1 positions with significant scholarships. But in each case, in widely different settings, they were both unhappy. Yes, they could compete with their team, but they couldn't find the positive dynamic to build their confidence and fulfillment. Why didn't I ask more questions or act as a better detective? Why didn't I see the risks, the shortcomings, and the potential downsides? Why was I swept away by the packaging only to miss the realities of the experience that I authorized my children to pursue?

With these experiences as motivation, we set out to make it easier for you and your family to better view the Division 1 (D1) experience, before you finish recruitment and sign the binding commitment. We wanted to create the resource that I wish we had when we started this journey, so that you will have clarity and breadth of perspective; so that you will have tools to better understand the typical routines in the colleges you review; so that your athlete will find an experience that allows him or her to thrive personally, socially, academically and athletically.

This book is a compilation of the personal stories of 60 current, or recently graduated, D1 athletes. They represent various sports and schools of all sizes across the United States. We trained two interviewers, both former D1 athletes, to solicit stories from athletes following a common protocol and format (*See Appendix for Research Protocol*). The anecdotes and insights gathered have been modified for clarity and grammar only, these are THEIR WORDS.

So, this is your chance to listen to 60 D1 athletes who have successfully navigated the recruiting challenges, obtained a roster spot, and lived the D1 experience ...

Please let their experiences help you gain clarity on the D1 landscape and routine. Armed with the insights of 60 committed athletes, it is our hope that you can more carefully and purposefully find the right program, coach, and team to make your child's college athletic experience the dream you are hoping for ... and the dream that he or she deserves.

Our views on college athletic recruiting today

We have witnessed many rising high school athletes who are so enthralled with the hope to play "against all odds" that they forget to think beyond the sport and consider the overall college experience that will provide well-rounded preparation for life. Perhaps like you, or like your athlete, these aspiring athletes relentlessly attend recruiting camps and showcase tournaments; they make websites and videos to "sell" themselves; and they sit anxiously by the phone hoping that a coach might call. They answer endless neighborly inquiries asking if they've heard anything or committed anywhere. They are so overwhelmed with the competition to win the game of college athletic recruiting, that they often lose sight of the bigger experience that college provides as a foundation for almost all aspects of life.

College can be (and should be!) more than an opportunity to play sport or an extension of the high school experience. College should be a canvas of many challenges --- personal, athletic, academic and social --- to help broaden and refine an individual's potential and goals. College should be a strong foundation for moving forward, on sure feet, into life beyond classrooms and playing fields. And while athletics is a great component for some students, the competitive recruiting maze often distracts athletes and families from the real goals and value of the overall college experience.

No doubt, there can be great athletic benefits in securing a coveted spot as a college athlete, and especially if you make it to the infamous level of D1. As an athlete, you will learn about team dynamics and teamwork, which can position you for better collaboration in the future. You will learn time management and the art of balancing practice, travel, games and academic requirements. You will learn self-discipline and grit, as pushing through the pain and exhaustion of one practice, only to get ready for the next. You might even observe an incredible coach who can be a role model for leadership in the rest of your life. All these things might happen, if you actually, and most deliberately, search out the right environment, team, and coach that fit your personal needs, desires and potential.

But, there are other questions to consider. Will the time commitment and pressure of a D1 athletic environment allow you the opportunity to excel academically? Find friends beyond athletes? Explore clubs, internships or jobs that will prepare you for a satisfying career? Will your coach and teammates help you thrive both within and beyond your sport? Will athletics be just a part of your college experience? Or, will sport become the sole focus and driver in college, causing you to lose sight of other great opportunities present in a college experience? These are the questions to sort through during the recruiting process. This is the purpose of this book.

This book does not presume to provide an easy path to the right answer, or to change the college athletic recruiting process or experience. Rather, it is an attempt to help you and your family think beyond recruiting, to life as an athlete. It is meant to improve your understanding of the D1 athletic experience, and to help you realize that you have options in making a selection to best fit your personal, athletic, academic and social needs. Remember the saying, "hindsight is 20/20"? We set out to bring you that kind of clarity.

This book conveys the insight and realities of 60 D1 athletes so that you can 'try on' their experiences and see how their reality might influence your understanding and selection. This book also includes a set of tools that might help broaden your thinking about your ideal college experience, and heighten your observations of the programs you are considering. The book represents the commitment of several athletes and their parents to give you the best chance of a happy, healthy and fulfilling experience in college, both within and beyond athletics.

Congratulations on being ready for college athletics. We wish you options and clear choices to fulfill your dreams.

Introduction

When an athlete embarks on securing a spot in college athletics, the experience can be overwhelming and confusing for everyone in the family. It is a high-pressure process that starts as early as freshman year in high school, way before the natural college application process begins, so even basic preparation in evaluating the potential college experience is lost. Conversations with college-seeking varsity athletes often shift toward pushing the most competitive athletic options, instead of an overall good college match. Sometimes relationships with formerly trusted coaches and teammates become strained as everyone is jockeying for a precious few positions. Amidst a plethora of NCAA rules and accepted (but cryptic) workarounds, parents and students are engaged in trying to navigate a maze from the very start. And because athletes are competitive by nature, the idea of "winning the most competitive spot" often overshadows the notion of evaluating the college's academic, social and athletic opportunities to find a match that will bring out your personal best.

There is wholesome truth in the adage that "hindsight is 20/20." With that in mind, we thought that if rising athletes and families could gain a better understanding of what happens after recruiting in the day-to-day life of Division 1 (D1) college athletes, they could work backwards to make better choices in their own selection process.

We are hopeful that exploring the stories of 60 D1 athletes will help you determine your personal hopes and priorities, and focus your ability to make keen observations during the recruiting process. Perhaps, a greater understanding of the D1 landscape will encourage you to ask deeper questions and engage in thoughtful critique of available options, despite the pressure and hype of competition.

Building your perspective and understanding of what happens after recruiting, in the real lives of D1 athletes, is the ultimate goal of this book. Equipped with 'real life' insight and reflection, you can ultimately make a more informed and effective college decision. Congratulations on your achievements thus far! Getting to the edge of the college arena has required great work and sacrifice – you are quite amazing to have arrived at this point.

We would appreciate your input on the usefulness of this book, so please see the last section of the appendix and send us your thoughts at **d1dream.info@gmail.com**.

Good luck in the pages ahead … and the college visits that follow … and the seasons that let your dreams come true.

How to Best Use This Book

The pages ahead are a combination of insights shared by experienced D1 athletes, and tools to help you apply these insights in a way that best makes sense for you. By working through the details, we hope that you will find an athletic experience that matches your athletic talent, as well as your hopes and dreams. Wishing you the best in recruiting and beyond!

1. Congratulations! And, This is Hard
    Insights – the differences between high school and college athletics

2. Begin With the End in Mind
    Insights – the best of times and lessons learned
    Considerations:
    - **Worksheet:** My personal bests and worsts
    - **Worksheet:** What do I value most in my sport?
    - **Worksheet:** Learning from their lessons learned

3. Find Your Winning Context
    Insights – coaches, team dynamics, and social life of D1 athletes
    Considerations:
    - **Worksheet:** What do I really want in college?
    - **Worksheet:** What do I want in my college coach?
    - **Worksheet:** Focus on four!

4. Know the Risks
    Insights – the worst of times for these D1 athletes
    Considerations:
    - **Worksheet:** Am I prepared for the worst?

5. Prepare for Academic Practicalities
    Insights – academics, professors and career preparation
    Considerations:
    - **Worksheet:** Thinking through my academic success
    - **Research Input:** Consider the realities of getting a job

6. Plan for Common Challenges
    Insights – handling the tough times: injuries, homesickness, travel, etc.
    Considerations:
    - **Worksheet:** Can I realistically handle potential challenges and still personally win?

7. Informed Recruiting: Finding a Great Match
    Insights -- parent to parent, and athlete to athlete
    Considerations:
    - **Worksheet:** Athlete questions and observations during recruiting
    - **Worksheet:** Parent assignments for recruiting visits
    - **Worksheet:** Tips for researching athletic programs

*For ebook readers, please email **d1dream.info@gmail.com** for a PDF version of all worksheets included in this book.*

1

Congratulations! And, This is Hard ...

You have worked very hard, and it's impressive that you're considering college athletics! Congratulations on achieving this level of athleticism, and congratulations on aspiring to do even more.

There are approximately 8 million athletes in high school, many (or perhaps most) that hope to continue playing sports in college. Less than 7% will have a chance to play in college, and less than 3% will have a chance to play at the coveted level called D1. These statistics reflect all sports, not just the TV ready football and basketball teams. It is really difficult for anyone to get the opportunity to play college sport – from track, to lacrosse; from field hockey to rowing; so congratulations to you for being in the pipeline. Here's a look at the numbers:

Regarding High School Sports
Enrollment in high school sports has been steadily increasing since 2000[1]:

	Male Participation	Female Participation	Total Participation
2000-01	3,921,069	2,784,154	6,705,223
2001-02	3,960,517	2,806,998	6,767,515
2002-03	3,988,738	2,856,358	6,845,096
2003-04	4,038,253	2,865,299	6,903,552
2004-05	4,110,310	2,908,390	7,018,709
2005-06	4,206,549	2,953,355	7,159,904
2006-07	4,321,103	3,021,807	7,342,910
2008-09	4,372,115	3,057,266	7,429,381
2009-10	4,422,622	3,114,091	7,536,753
2010-11	4,455,740	3,172,637	7,628,377
2011-12	4,494,406	3,207,533	7,692,520
2012-13	4,490,854	3,222,723	7,713,577
2013-14	4,527,994	3,267,664	7,795,658
2014-15	4,519,312	3,287,735	7,807,047

---

[1] National Federation of State High School Associations, 2014-15 Athletics Participation Summary;

The most popular high school programs based on overall athlete participation as of 2014-2015 are as follows[2]:

Male Sport	
Football – 11 Player	1,083,617
Track and Field - Outdoor	578,632
Basketball	541,479
Baseball	486,567
Soccer	432,569
Wrestling	258,208
Cross Country	250,981
Tennis	157,240
Golf	148,823
Swimming and Diving	137,087

Female Sport	
Track and Field - Outdoor	478,726
Volleyball	432,176
Basketball	429,504
Soccer	375,681
Softball – Fast Pitch	364,103
Cross Country	221,616
Tennis	182,876
Swimming and Diving	166,838
Competitive Spirit Squads	125,763
Lacrosse	84,785

---

[2] National Federation of State High School Associations, 2014-15 Athletics Participation Summary; http://www.nfhs.org/ParticipationStatistics/PDF/2014-15_Participation_Survey_Results.pdf

Estimated Probability of Competing in College

According to the NCAA website in November 2016, the estimated probability of competing in college athletics is quite low[3], as indicated in the center column in the following chart. If it's truly your dream, then you will find your spot. Be smart and persistent. But, if you're not 110% sure that you want to be committed, then step back and take time to consider not just the recruiting challenges, but the ongoing challenges relayed by the athlete stories in this book.

	High School Participants	NCAA Participants	Overall % HS to NCAA	% HS to NCAA Division I	% HS to NCAA Division II	% HS to NCAA Division III
Men						
Baseball	486,567	34,198	**7.0%**	2.1%	2.2%	2.7%
Basketball	541,479	18,697	**3.5%**	1.0%	1.0%	1.4%
Cross Country	250,981	14,330	**5.7%**	1.9%	1.4%	2.3%
Football	1,083,617	72,788	**6.7%**	2.6%	1.8%	2.4%
Golf	148,823	8,654	**5.8%**	2.0%	1.7%	2.1%
Ice Hockey	35,875	4,071	**11.3%**	4.6%	0.5%	6.3%
Lacrosse	108,450	13,165	**12.1%**	2.9%	2.2%	7.1%
Soccer	432,569	24,477	**5.7%**	1.3%	1.5%	2.8%
Swimming	137,087	9,715	**7.1%**	2.8%	1.1%	3.2%
Tennis	157,240	8,211	**5.2%**	1.7%	1.1%	2.4%
Track & Field	578,632	28,177	**4.9%**	1.9%	1.2%	1.7%
Volleyball	54,418	1,818	**3.3%**	0.7%	0.8%	1.8%
Water Polo	21,626	1,044	**4.8%**	2.6%	0.7%	1.5%
Wrestling	258,208	7,049	**2.7%**	1.0%	0.7%	1.0%
Women						
Basketball	429,504	16,589	**3.9%**	1.2%	1.1%	1.6%
Cross Country	221,616	16,150	**7.3%**	2.7%	1.7%	2.8%
Field Hockey	60,549	5,894	**9.7%**	2.9%	1.2%	5.7%
Golf	72,582	5,221	**7.2%**	3.0%	2.1%	2.1%
Ice Hockey	9,418	2,175	**23.1%**	9.0%	1.1%	13.1%
Lacrosse	84,785	10,994	**13.0%**	3.7%	2.5%	6.7%
Soccer	375,681	26,995	**7.2%**	2.4%	1.9%	2.9%
Softball	364,103	19,628	**5.4%**	1.7%	1.6%	2.1%
Swimming	166,838	12,428	**7.4%**	3.2%	1.1%	3.1%
Tennis	182,876	8,960	**4.9%**	1.6%	1.1%	2.2%
Track & Field	478,726	28,797	**6.0%**	2.7%	1.5%	1.8%
Volleyball	432,176	17,026	**3.9%**	1.2%	1.2%	1.6%
Water Polo	19,204	1,152	**6.0%**	3.5%	1.1%	1.4%

---

[3] http://www.ncaa.org/about/resources/research/estimated-probability-competing-college-athletics

Scholarships – The Lucky 2%

There is a widespread popular belief that college athletes, in general, are on scholarship for their sport. There is sometimes a sense that they are a 'privileged' group. While it is an honor to play sports for your chosen university, it is not usually accompanied by a scholarship. Very few athletes will receive a full scholarship, or even a significant scholarship, so let's be real; this is not the ticket to a free education. At the time of this writing, the NCAA reports that only about 2% of high school athletes are awarded athletic scholarships to compete in college.[4]

- Division III schools do not offer athletic scholarships.
- Division I includes 176,000 student athletes in 346 colleges and universities. Approximately 56% of all student athletes receive some level of athletic aid (ranging from book money to full tuition).[5]
- Division II schools include about 118,800 athletes in 307 colleges and universities. Approximately 61% of all student athletes receive some level of athletic aid.[6]

The statistics are sobering, but they are the reality you must consider as you embark on this journey. Many students, like you, continue rigorous training and endure competitive, exhausting recruiting, because it is their hope to join a team, be mentored by a coach, wear the gear, and make the fans proud. Far too many high school students get swept up in the recruiting process without conducting enough research, asking enough questions, and doing enough personal searching and discovery. Many high school athletes have dedicated their focus to playing in college -- a dream come true -- so getting there becomes the goal without considering what comes after signing day.

Interestingly, despite the odds, getting on the team is the easy part. The four years that follow can be thrilling, fulfilling and exhausting. This book is meant to help you take off the blinders during recruiting and assess your options, so that you find the best match to meet your personal choices and goals.

---

[4] http://www.ncaa.org/student-athletes/future/scholarships
[5] http://www.ncaa.org/sites/default/files/Recruiting%20Fact%20Sheet%20WEB.pdf (as of 3.18.17)
[6] Same as above

Stories about the Shift to College Sports
Insights from D1 athletes about the differences between high school and college athletics

The following stories were collected during our interviews with 60 D1 athletes. These are shared in their exact words, with minimal editing, just as if they were sitting and talking directly to you. Here's what they have to say ...

Like High School on Steroids
"I have honestly told the girls at my high school asking about playing in college, that college is like high school but on steroids. I do not mean this in a bad way at all. I simply mean that you give up a lot of time, sweat, and tears in high school athletics, but in college, you give up more. It is a real commitment. You don't get to go out and live the basic college life, but you do get to be part of something amazing, a team dedicated to playing the sport you love."

New Routines
"The biggest difference relating to my sport is how it changed from entirely an individual sport to a team sport. For the first time in my life at college, I had teammates beside me cheering me on and supporting me. Another thing that is definitely different is that in high school, I had my parents, and now, in college, they are an 8-hour drive away. Without them, I was forced to learn how to be much more independent and handle issues on my own (and also handle money, rent, groceries, etc.). A final difference is the change in workouts, as for 17 years I was used to working out a specific way with my coach at home, and immediately, once I came to college, I was forced to forget these workouts and accept the new ones."

Intense Training and Competition
"The biggest difference, athletically speaking, is the training and the competition for playing time. The preseason training (lifting and conditioning) in high school was practically nonexistent. In college the training is an all year, incredibly intense, and an exhausting aspect of D1 athletics that I didn't consider that much before I made my decision to play. The level of competition in high school was very low. Playing time was guaranteed, and there wasn't much competition when it came to teams and players we'd play against. In college, everyone is competing for the playing time and it becomes a cutthroat job. Every player I play with and against is big, strong, and athletic. In high school that was hardly the case."

All on YOU
"Academics are no joke in college. High school academics are a joke compared to the college workload, and the density of the subject matter. Responsibility is another big one. YOU are responsible for all your success and failure whether that is academically or in athletics. You are an adult in college, and no matter what year you are, that is how you will be expected to act...as an adult! Free time is rarely free."

90%/10%
"When it comes to percentages, in high school it was like 50% school and 50% golf. In college it was 90% golf and 10% school. Everyone knows you by your specific sports team. People know what team you are associated with. There's a lot more structure."

Individual Competitiveness
"College is a next level step, because in college, you are literally sacrificing your body and everything for the team. It is way more intense than high school. It is another jump. High school maybe gives you a little taste of the schedule and the routine of practice everyday and games, but college really brings out the competitiveness in individuals. At times it is really hard to balance the competitiveness and perfectionism that can be brought out of a person. In my experience, it's important to have people that you trust. That's why the relationship between coach and athlete needs to be very strong. Players going into the program need to ask the hard questions before they get there, like how much playing time can I expect?"

It's a Job
"High school athletics don't consume your life. They are lower level. It hasn't weeded out the people who are not going to play in college or the stars who are going to go all the way in sport. There is a lot bigger range of players making it a little bit more fun and less serious and pressured. I think college sports are a business. It is a job. It can be a fun job, but it is work."

It Takes Hours Every Day
"In high school you have a lot of class, and only some sport. In college you have some class, and a lot of sport! You're living with teammates, you have random athletic meetings, and you have many film sessions. If we had film, I wouldn't get out of there until 5:30 or 6:00pm. I think just the fact that they are able to keep you for hours a day, for film, for anything -- makes it more of an adjustment."

Sports Come First
"Everything is different! In high school, academics come first, because you have to have the grades to get recruited. In college, I'd say it's quite the opposite. You're expected to just deal with school and pass while excelling on the court."

A Lot More Than I'm Used To
"Academically I didn't try in high school, I just cruised by. That's just how it was. College put me on it, back peddling in a way. It's just a lot more work than I am used to, but you figure it out pretty quickly. Swimming wise, college is more swimming than I had ever done. It was a lot more work for me when I got to college. I wasn't used to morning practices or anything like that."

Pressure, Intensity, Time Management
"I would say that you have to be a lot more efficient with your time, and really manage your time effectively in college because of the courses. There is really no easy major, and if you don't pass your classes, you won't be able to compete-- so there's that extra motivation to pass your class. Being efficient, and being able to manage your time is super important, and then I guess challenging yourself on and off the field. Just the mentality towards football and school is a lot more intense. There is a lot more pressure obviously."

Your thoughts about their stories?
What matches your expectations?
What surprises you?
… What will work for you?

> *"Begin with the end in mind. Start with the end outcome and work backwards to make your dream possible."*
> -Wayne W. Dyer

2

Begin With the End in Mind

D1 college athletics is often a collection of radical opposites. For some, it is the launching pad to education and confidence that they never dreamed possible. For others, it is a match gone completely wrong, that creates quite the opposite of physical and mental well-being.

But for you, it should be the dream that you want. That means, knowing what's important to you, and determining how that matches the options available. Your recruiting process should not be a quick match with a recommended program, but a thoughtful search for an environment that matches your personal, social, academic and athletic goals.

Based on our interviews with 60 D1 athletes, let's take a look at what they have experienced, as a way to help you more clearly articulate what you are hoping for and what you can manage in college sport.

- **Best Memories** – athlete stories that confirm the tremendous value and bonds that can be part of the right college athletic experience

- **Lessons Learned** – looking back at the total experience, what will be remembered and impact your life

Before you read their stories,
What are your hopes for college athletics?

Best memories of current or former D1 athletes...

Personal Best!
"Our team has this joke that our coach isn't much of a hugger. My sophomore year it was our outdoor championships, and I doubled in the Steeplechase and the 5k. I had only ever run one 5k on the track in my entire running career. I had a goal in mind, and after a long talk with my coach before the race, her only message was, 'you are one of the most talented athletes I have coached and I just know you have something great inside of you today.' I ended up running a HUGE personal record and as I crossed the finish line, my coach was sprinting towards the finish line to hug me. This was one of my favorite moments."

Record Breaking
"The best memory of my athletic career would be winning the conference and making it to the NCAA tournament. We ended up breaking some school and conference records as well as making the team's first NCAA appearance in 20 years. We received a great deal of publicity and respect from members of our school and community. It was an amazing thing to be a part of."

Best Friends
"My best memory of playing Division 1 lacrosse is doing everything with my best friends. While this sounds corny, my teammates are truly my best friends, in addition to being the people that I live with, hang out with, and basically do everything with. Everything we do, whether it's 6am workouts, 12-hour bus rides, or staying in on weekend game nights, we make the best of every situation and have fun doing it. For example, during the spring, we can't go out on Friday or Saturday nights because we have games the next day, so we have made it mandatory game night, and we invite all of our friends over to play games like Catch Phrase and Charades. Sounds pretty lame, but I have never laughed harder or had more fun."

Family Away From Home
"Besides just being able to play the game I love, my best experiences from this past year are the times with my teammates when I truly got to know them. The joking around in the locker room, the serious discussions on what we can do to grow as a team, and even the tears from outside the court have allowed me to grow closer to the team I'm on now. They have become my family away from home, and I wouldn't trade that for anything."

Opportunities and Support
"Some of the best memories I have made during my Division 1 athletic experience happened on our trips. Our team has traveled to many places around the country; we are in Hawaii right now, and I have had the opportunity to experience many things that I would not have gotten to without being a Division 1 athlete. Some of my best experiences have been with the people at my school that work to assist athletes: tutors, advisors, professors and coaches. From my experience, athletes are very well provided for, and if you are willing to ask, you will gain a lot of helpful advice."

First Win in 3 Years
"My best memory is when we won our first conference game. I have never been part of an experience like that before. We had not won a conference game in 3 years, and then we finally did it! It was the most satisfying experience I have ever been part of. You honestly would have thought we won the national championship; everybody was jumping up and down. The feeling that I did something to help my team win was better than anything in the world."

Doing the Seemingly Impossible
"My best memory of my Division 1 experience was making school and program history with my team last conference season. Our team has for many years been looked at as the underdog of our conference, and last season we all came together and contributed to achieve the best conference record in school history. Within two years our team improved from being last in the conference, to second, yet, with one more win and we would have been first. Knowing we had done something for the program that had never been done before was an incredible feeling and personally, made me even more determined to develop my game so that I can make history again in my next years by leading my team to a conference championship."

Traveling
"Best memories, by far, are traveling. Whether it is a flight or a bus ride, the time with the guys traveling is like nothing else. I mean they say couples that can travel together stay together, and the same goes for a team. We have a roommate system so that you are always with the same position group, but not necessarily the same person. Playing games is great and so is winning, but the time you get to spend seeing new places, new hotels, schools, airports, environments ... it's like nothing else. In my opinion it is what really builds a team, and adds to the chemistry as a whole."

Synergy
"My best memory with my team would be our summer trip to Germany. We played 4 games there. The most exciting part was when we played a professional reserves

team. We beat them 4 to 2! The talent of the team was unreal, but our team just had one of those games where we played out of our minds. That was the moment we realized we had a very good chance to win the national championship that upcoming season, considering that was only our second game of the trip with less than a week of practicing together. The whole trip in general was one of my all time favorite personal memories, not just soccer related. I'll cherish that memory for the rest of my life."

Earning My First Start
"My best memory was definitely earning my first start as a Division 1 athlete. There's just so much I had to go through personally to get there. There were times that I asked myself why I was continuing to do this, because I was putting in so much work, but I wasn't finding the reward. I thought I should just move onto my next chapter and really focus on life after athletics. Looking back on it, hearing that I was going to start my first game at my school was definitely my best memory."

Living My Dream
"For me, it was all great memories because it was what I made it. My time at my school was truly sensational. It was a dream. I was living full-heartedly my dream. I could've gone to a lesser school my freshman year with a full scholarship, but I chose to follow my gut. My heart was with the school that I chose. I was beyond grateful and still so grateful for that experience. Those same friends are still some of my very close friends today, which is awesome."

Proving Myself
"It was my junior year when I was at the point where I was fed up with my coaches. They weren't pushing me to be the best I could be. They would just put me on the field and tell me to do my thing. So, I picked up the team, put them up on my shoulders, and stepped up my game for my team. I ended up getting the Defensive Player of the Year, which was nice because before that, my coach didn't believe in me at all. When I went to his office to tell him the news he had a look on his face that suggested he didn't believe me. He told me not to let it get to my head. That was one of my favorite moments because I was able to prove to my coach that I was worthy of being on the field and being a Division 1 player. I totally showed him that I was better than he thought I was."

Against the Odds
"My favorite memory is my sophomore year. I played forward, because my coach said that I didn't know how to play defense. My dad came to my game for the first time in over a year. I got into the game off the bench, because my coach got pissed at one of the forwards on the field. Five minutes into the game I scored a goal, and then seven

*minutes later I scored again. We were up 2-0. It was just a great moment because my coach had been so hard on me. It was really cool to be like, F*** you, you can treat me poorly but I'm still going to do my thing. That was probably my best moment."*

Bonding
"The offensive linemen every year take a weekend retreat to Tennessee and we hang out with each other away from football. It's bonding time, and we just hang out together. This is a time when we can get away, since we pretty much train year round."

Service
"I think my best memory of my Division 1 experience was the service we participated in every Saturday morning. We would drive to a soccer academy for children with special needs and spend an hour coaching them and playing with them. The best part was that our coach didn't come. Her presence was always a bit suffocating and fake in my eyes. Without her there, I could smile again, and these kids helped to bring me back to reality. It was nice to see families again, and kids who loved soccer. I was so desperate and so longing to feel like that again."

Shared Struggle
"I had a great relationship with my teammates. I have a bunch of friends that play DI, DII, and DIII sports in college. I would say that my team is not as close as say a DIII team is, just because we have such a bigger team, which I think, makes it a bit more of a clique with certain groups within the team. But overall, I am happy with the relationships I have with my teammates. I had a certain small group of guys that I was closest with. You know, we really bonded through all the trials and tribulations, and hardships that we go through together, the job of being a Division 1 athlete. But it's because of the shared struggle that we are so close."

Just Plain Fun
"During cross country regionals my sophomore year there was a moment I will never forget. It was the day before the race and the team had just finished jogging the course and it was COLD that day. We all hustled to the van and waited for our coaches to finish up their meeting. While we were waiting, we blasted some music and were dancing and singing and just letting any stress fall away. We were shaking the van and fogging the windows and it was just a memory that shows the fun our team can have!"

Lessons learned from current or former D1 athletes...

Stick it Out
"I think being an athlete has helped me to learn to stick something out and work hard. But I do feel like I have missed out a lot on educating myself more broadly. I really have started to enjoy school, but I am usually too tired to want to learn extra, or to go to career fairs. I think for me personally, I skip a lot of things that would help me with my career. It was more my own doing, than because of soccer."

Social Skills
"I've grown so much as a person because of golf. Looking back from freshman year to now is insane. Dealing with stress was my biggest issue coming into freshman year. Now, I've learned how to cope with it. It's a lot easier for me to let things go. It's gotten me more open to communicating, and to be a little bit more extroverted."

Courage and Empathy
"I think my Division 1 experience has made me a stronger person, but the scars and bruises run deep. Building the courage to stand up for myself in such an oppressive environment was a great challenge. My confidence, self-esteem, and passion for soccer and school was taken from me, and it took a huge toll on my character and personality. I have now recovered, and I can thank my family, my new school, and my new teammates and friends who stood by my side and helped me to find my happiness again. However, there are still times in class, on the field, or in job interviews when I doubt my ability because of the lasting traces of emotional and physical abuse. My experience will always be a part of me. In many ways it has shaped who I am and who I want to be. I will never treat others how I was treated by my coach and her athletic staff. I will never stand by and watch another's dignity and humanity be taken from them. Nothing in life is worth that."

Learning to be More
"Of course the experience of it made me into the person that I am -- like scheduling, prioritizing, being busy all the time, and exercising. I think for a long time Division 1 sports were in line with my values of being healthy, and being busy, and being successful, and making it in the world and being useful. The experience of being an athlete for two years definitely contributed to the person that I am. I also think quitting and spending two years without sports was really important. I think I almost grew more in those two years alone. I used all those skills that I gained as an athlete to be a better teacher, to graduate, to work on my GPA, and to run a marathon. It goes both ways. I think you just have to use the experience for what you need."

Handling Tough Conversations
"Sports help so much with learning how to talk to people and have hard conversations. At the age of 12, I had to go talk to a coach to ask why I didn't play in a State Cup game. A lot of people don't learn that until they are older and facing a boss. Also injury wise, you have to learn how to take care of yourself, and how to make relationships with people. Everything about college sports has improved me as a person."

Self Esteem From Within
"You're going to have good days and bad days. The good days give you a boost. You come to realize that confidence and self-esteem comes from within. It's not something that someone can give you. You learn that through your sport."

Working Together Despite Differences
"I think it has made me a better person. I've faced things in soccer that I wouldn't have faced otherwise. I've dealt with people that I wouldn't have dealt with otherwise. I've learned to work with people who aren't necessarily like me outside of soccer, which you can translate into the real world. Just because you aren't all the same person doesn't mean you can't work together to accomplish a similar goal together."

Role Models: Good and Bad
"Playing for a coach like I had in college, I am 100% confident that I will never have another boss more stupid, and more unreasonable than him. My coach has demonstrated to me what not to be when I enter the professional workplace/ world."

The Chance to be a Student
"As miserable as my experience was athletically, I can say with the utmost confidence that I took advantage of the academic opportunities. I will never forget the great conversations I had with my peers and professors and my internship. I wish I could do it all over again and just be a student."

Time Management
"My experience has definitely made me a better person. Playing college sports has given me great time management skills. It makes me strategically plan everything. If I have a paper due Sunday, I do it Wednesday when I have time, whereas regular students tend to do it the night before. It has also made me realize not to take things so personally. You can't let it consume your life. It turned me into someone who uses criticism in a positive light."

Survive Despite Challenges
"It definitely helps with the work place. I don't think I'll ever deal with a boss that treats me as bad as my first coach did. I feel like I am prepared for the worst. That's one positive side of it. I also think that being on a team you learn tolerance, and how to deal with people that you don't necessarily want to deal with. I think that's a great quality. That's a sign of maturity. You are not going to like everything about everyone and you're not going to like everyone. There are also the little things, like persevering through the hard stuff. When you reach adversity it's fight or flight, and I think athletes tend to choose to fight."

Gratitude and Acceptance
"Absolutely, it has made me a better person. Coming into this experience I had a poor me attitude, and I've realized that there is nothing to gain from self-pity. There is no single person that doesn't struggle. You cannot put yourself on any pedestal that says you have it harder. You gain perspective on those days when you don't want to be out there doing your sport, and you start to think about how lousy it felt when you were injured and you couldn't perform. You learn to live in the moment. You learn to appreciate the time that you have. You learn time management. You learn respect. You learn teamwork and collaboration. You learn a lot of humility. I'm serious when I say that. You learn acceptance."

Mental Strength and Independence
"I have gone through a lot of different things that I can speak to. Life isn't easy, so some of the hard things I went through made me a stronger person. I wouldn't say they prepared me for the work force, but I do think I am mentally stronger and more independent. Workwise, I thankfully was in a city that made having a job easily accessible. If I hadn't been, I would feel very behind not having a job going into the workforce. Being an athlete can only take you so far. People in the workforce don't always really understand how much time and energy you put into your sport unless they were an athlete too."

Humility
"It has made me a much more humble person. I think when you come from high school and you're going to play a Division 1 sport, I think it's very easy to think highly of yourself. Realistically, you are one of the better players at your school. You think you're awesome, but then you get to college and you realize that the ten other players in your recruiting class were also the best players from their area. It's like big fish, small pond; but now you are in an ocean. You realize that there is so much talent out

there, and that if you want to make your mark, you need to work extremely hard. That's translated academically as well. I think being pre-med, which is very competitive, if you really want to be a doctor, you need to put in the work to have a shot."

Value of Hard Work, Despite Pressure
"Yes, I have improved as a person being a college athlete. I would say that I have learned how to perform under pressure and make decisions under pressure. I learned how to work as a team and with the team—just learning the value of hard work."

For Your Consideration ...

Your thoughts about their stories?
What matches your expectations?
What surprises you?
… What will work for you?

Worksheet: Personal Bests and Worsts

You can often anticipate what you need by reflecting on the highs and lows from the past. Complete this table including as many memories as you can, but you must have at least one high and one low for each year. Review your entries to see what makes you strong, and what brings you down. Keep these on your radar during your conversations and visits with potential colleges.

	Think through your experiences in high school and club athletics ...	
	What made you happy & strong: **"Bests"**	What brought you down: **"Worsts"**
Freshman Year		
Sophomore Year		
Junior Year		
Senior Year		

Additional notes on your personal bests and worsts ...

Worksheet: What do you VALUE MOST in playing sports?

Overview: Why do you love your sport? What is it that propels you through the hard practices, the gut-wrenching losses, the painful injuries, and the never-ending exhaustion? Different athletes participate for different reasons. Knowing what you value about your sport will help you find a program that values the same things. Just like finding the perfect job, you need to look at how the athletic environment fits with what you value most.

Instructions: Review each of the items in the following list. Identify how you value each item: high, medium or low. Then, rank your high-priority values in order from 1-5.

Scoring: Keep these values at the core of your radar during your conversations and visits with potential colleges.

Things you value in athletics	Your Priority High, Medium or Low	Ranking Which are your top 5?
• Trusted relationship with coach		
• Trusted teammates		
• Physical challenge		
• Competition		
• Winning		
• Routine and discipline		
• Love of the game		
• Recognition for being an athlete		
• Scholarship potential		
• Potential to play professionally		
• Carrying on the family legacy		
• Being a starting member (top competitor) of the team		
• Being captain		
• Playing in the games/meets etc.		
• Being part of a team, even if I don't play/compete		
What would you add?		
•		
•		
•		
•		
	Are these possible?	

Additional thoughts on what you value in your sport …

Worksheet: Learning From Their Lessons Learned

The athletes interviewed shared lessons learned for each of the following topics. What do these lessons mean to you?	
Improve My Social Skills	
Work as a Team	
Handle Tough Issues	
Find My Self Esteem from Within	
Work Together Despite Differences	
Recognize Role Models, Good and Bad	
Enjoy Being a Student	
Learn Time Management	
Stick it Out; Survive Despite Challenges	
Practice Gratitude and Acceptance	
Build Mental Strength and Independence	
Work Effectively Under Pressure	
Learn to be More	
Build Courage and Empathy	
What Else?	

> *"Culture is defined and created from the top down, but it comes to life from the bottom up."*
>
> –Mike Smith
> Defensive Coordinator for the Tampa Bay Buccaneers
> Former Head Coach of the Atlanta Falcons

3
Find Your Winning Context

Perhaps the biggest factors impacting your happiness in college athletics will be your relationships with your coach and team. Win or lose, on the field or off, training or competition, if you are energized and supported by these people, you will probably find happiness as a college athlete. With this perspective, you need to review your potential coaches and teammates objectively, to discern if they are a good match for you. This takes the ability to know what you want, and to look past the sugarcoating of the recruiting pitch into the reality and climate of the team during its normal routine.

Based on our interviews with 60 D1 athletes, let's take a look at what they have experienced, as a way to help you more clearly articulate what you are hoping for, and what you can manage, in college athletics.

- **Coaches** – Athletes share the realities of working with coaches who are under contract to produce winning results in D1. What happens when their livelihood depends on creating team performance to win championships?

- **Team** – When the competition escalates, team dynamics are more difficult to predict. This section includes honest and true descriptions of what has actually happened on and off the playing field, court, track etc.

- **Social Life** – Here are a few reflections about off the field activities; integrating activities beyond school and sports.

Before you read their stories,
What are your hopes...
- **For your coach?**
- **For your team?**
- **For your social life?**

Stories about D1 Coaches
Insights from D1 athletes about their experiences working with coaches

Disconnected
"Literally the only time I see my coach is during practice. She knows nothing about any of us. She can be a bully when she says cruel comments that are 85% of the time unnecessary. Since there is no relationship with her, it's hard to accept that she means well, because we don't know if her mean comments are actually coming from a place of caring for us. I have been here for four years and she knows nothing about me and I don't know anything about her."

More Like a Manager
"My head coach feels more like a manager. He's very demanding and stern, but not like a yeller. You can tell he's frustrated just by the tone of his voice. I have never been that close with him in the sense that I only have two minute conversations with him, and I'm going into my 4th year with him. The only time we have long conversations is when it comes to school and soccer. However, I do feel that if I have an issue, he is someone I can reach out to. I trust his way of coaching and never have had much of an issue with his philosophy, but for some it's really difficult to deal with him, because they don't feel connected with him."

Straight Talk
"My bad experiences were always during my meetings (with coach), because I usually had to fight to stay on the team. It was either because of academic issues or he just felt that I wouldn't play a lot. They were stressful, but I respected everything he told me in the meetings. I didn't think he was unjust in any of his meetings."

Rigid
"My coach's style is old style. She isn't about change. She doesn't like change in the golf game. I would say that she likes to stick with what she knows. She doesn't like to bring in other people, or hear a different view on what golf should be. She doesn't like outside input. Because of that, I am very protective of what I say to her, because she usually doesn't agree. I'm very hidden with my thoughts."

Practical Mentor
"What I liked about my coach is that he would apply life skills to soccer. He would always tell us to check our emails often, because in the real world that is what you do. He would say things to us like 'it is always in the details,' or 'it's in the little things.' He would always stop practice to point out certain players who were going above and beyond. It was very special."

Rollercoaster
"My relationship with my coach was very whimsical. I don't know if that is the right word, but it would fluctuate. Sometimes it was a good relationship, and sometimes it would be bad. It depended on what he needed from me, or if I was performing. I felt like it depended on whether I was a good player, rather than him actually liking me as a person. He didn't really hide his emotions very well."

Constructive
"My coach wouldn't come up to me to directly, but if I wanted to ask him something, he was always open to talk. It is always hard to talk to a coach. He was good about explaining things to us. He wouldn't tell you what you wanted to hear, but it would help you get better."

Financially Uptight
"My coach is very picky about his money. He would take advantage of local girls by giving them less scholarship money, and then he would recruit internationally and give those girls full scholarships. That was really tough on a lot of girls. He threatened scholarships on multiple occasions during end of season meetings. If someone asked for more money he would not be having it. I just feel like scholarships should be an open conversation with coaches rather than it being secretive or something."

Caring, But ...
"My relationship is different with my coach on and off the field. Off the field she is more of a friend. She definitely does care about us as people. She knows what's going on in our lives. She could tell you my siblings' names. She actually cares about us as people. It's awesome. However, she doesn't necessarily translate that onto the field. She'll tell you what you want to hear off the field about playing situations, but she's not really telling you exactly what she thinks about you as a player. She sugarcoats it, which sometimes gives you false hope. So she'll tell you that there's a chance of you playing and you won't."

Better Over Time
"I have a really great relationship with my coach, although it did not start there. It was never bad, but my first year as her athlete, we both didn't have much trust and faith in one another. Going into my sophomore year we had a really long conversation before departing for summer that got our relationship rolling. Now she isn't just a coach, she truly is a friend, and someone I often go to for advice (no matter the topic!). When I am freaking out about a workout, I have faith that I can do it because I know my coach believes that I can do it. It truly has turned into one of the best relationships I have."

Verbally Abusive
"I have seen my teammates almost tackled by my coach, and almost everyday, I listen to verbal abuse in the film room and on the field when someone messes up. He likes to mother F*** you when you mess up in a drill or in a play. He gets in your face to the point where his spit is all over your face."

No Good College Coach Memories
"I didn't really have a good experience with my first coach. And my coach now is very up-and-down, which may be part of their job. I wish I did have a close relationship with my coach, but I know he has a lot going on. I just don't really have good memories with any of my coaches. That being said, I am playing for my team and my teammates not my coach. My relationship with my teammates is more important."

Emotionally Charged
"I wish our coach talked to us more. He has a really bad problem of freaking out. This spring we lost the last two games of our season. We only had 11 field players, because everyone else was injured. The loss was 7-0. At the end of the game, he brought us all together. He said, 'I hope you know all of you are going to be replaced. All of you suck. I'm talking to a girl from Germany who is a professional goalie, and she'll take your position.' Then he was like, 'I have this girl to take your position, your position, your position,' while pointing at different girls. The team just felt like we had heard this so many times. He always tells us that we will be replaced. We wonder how that will make our team any better..."

Guilty Until Proven Innocent
"I would describe our relationship as guilty until proven innocent. When I came into school I wasn't on a scholarship. Coach had seen me play before and thought I could be a part of the team, but I don't think she ever thought that I would have a serious impact. I arrived to preseason being a nobody, having a torn ACL, and redshirting my freshman year. Sophomore year I wasn't starting at first, but I worked really hard to be part of the starting line up. And then I scored the penalty kick that led us to advance to the finals. And then the next year I was named captain. Coach would say good job if I did something really, really good, but my first year of competition we didn't really talk. Never did I go into her office to ask what I needed to do to get on the field. Never did she tell me I was going to be on the field. It was pretty much just work hard and be ready if you get the chance."

Not a People Manager
"Crazy. I don't even know her coaching style. That's how bad it was. I think that you need someone as a coach that knows how to manage people. If you don't know how to manage 18 to 22 year old women, then don't. It's not the job for you. I think she would be a great assistant coach, but as a head coach, I think she needed some administrative help."

Better Over Time
"I say that my relationship with my coach has definitely grown positively as time went on. When you get there from high school, you experience complete culture shock because football turns into a fulltime job where coaches are holding you accountable for everything. So, as a freshman you are like this is super intense, coach doesn't really care about me or what I do. But as I got older I started to see that the coaches actually really do care about you on and off the field. So I would say my relationship with my coach has strengthened, as I have gotten older."

No Nonsense
"My coach is very demanding. No nonsense. He tells you what he is thinking when he is thinking it, no exceptions. If you are playing poorly, you bet that you are going to hear about it. So it's definitely a very demanding coaching style. So like I said, as a freshman, a sophomore, even as a junior, it definitely takes getting used too. But as you get older, at least for me, I didn't want anything sugar coated because if someone tells you that you are doing great, but you are not getting the results you want, then you wonder what you are actually doing wrong."

Just Do Your Job
"He's very passionate. He is kind of old school but old school in the sense that I am an offensive lineman, so we are kind of like a thankless position. You go out there and do your job and are expected not to complain about it. You do it to the best of your abilities, and that is kind of how he coaches it. You have to be a hard hitting guy, that doesn't expect much in terms of compliments and rewards. Just do your job. Get it done."

Played Favorites
"I was recruited by a coach who ended up not being there when I finally arrived. I was on a full ride from the first coach, and then the new coach brought in all of her own recruits, and so she basically spent the season trying to bully me out of my scholarship. She was always very negative towards me, and she literally would not play me no matter what—even if I was playing great in practice. She was basically like no, you will never get a chance to play, and she openly told me that. She would tell me that I'd

never play over the girls coming in no matter how good I got, no matter how good I was. She said, 'I am not going to play you over them.'"

Believed in Everyone's Contribution
"Senior year, we got a new coach. I was pretty nervous about this because I didn't know who he was, and I didn't know if he was going to be better or worse than our old one. But he ended up being awesome. Because he believed in me, I feel like I played more. And even though a lot of times I didn't play, he still gave me the platform to be a leader on the team. I was voted team captain, and I was voted MVP my senior year, even being a player that did not really play that much. It was really more because he gave me the platform to say, hey even though I am not the best player on the team, I can still make the biggest impact. I really loved him as a coach. If it wasn't for him during my senior year I would have left volleyball hating it, never wanting to touch a volleyball again or anything. But because he showed me my worth again my senior year, he made a huge impact on me."

High Turnover
"I am pretty close with my current coach. We have had a few coaches over the past couple of years, but the one I have currently I do like. I have had a new coach every year in college. Losing coaches is pretty frustrating. We were all really upset when our first coach left freshman year because he had recruited us all. The second coach we had was a good coach but he was not very professional. Now we have the new one. He's pretty cool."

Not Good Enough
"The coach I was recruited by got fired the January before I reported for preseason my freshmen year. I actually flew to campus to meet my new coach, on my own time and money, right after she was hired. I really wanted to have a good relationship with her. But, she wasn't interested. I learned quickly that she had already recruited the next class and it was big incase any of the current freshmen decided to leave. It was clear from the beginning that she wanted nothing to do with us... she wanted her own players that she recruited to develop her own team. I didn't have even one great moment with my coach. Except for the day when she gave me permission to transfer. Then, I finally felt free...I felt like I got a little part of my humanity back. But, a great moment with her -- that never happened."

My Way or the Highway
"My coach likes things done his way... or get out. His way or the highway. One of his poorer qualities is that he judges your character from day one, and if you mess up ever, there are no second chances. You have one shot. He never forgets about anything. He never forgets if you drop a pass."

Things to Consider When You Meet A Prospective Coach:

- How is the coach interacting with the team? During games? During practice?
- How are athletes interacting with the coach? Is there positive, constructive conversation?
- Are the athletes actively receptive to input from the coach? Active receptivity would imply that there was a positive, trust-based relationship between the coach and that player.
- Does the coach address the athletes by name?
- What does the team say about the coach's interactions? Any moodiness?
- How do they describe what happens in coach/athlete meetings?
- How do the athletes describe the "best and worst" of the coach?

Stories about D1 Teams
Insights from D1 athletes about their experiences with teammates

Bonded Through Tragedy
"My junior year, I was elected captain in the spring. We had a really big set back because one of our teammates passed away. It was terrible. All 40 of us were really devastated. We used it to fuel us, and bind us together. We were all there for each other. We swam for him that year, and it was the biggest sense of brotherhood that I have ever experienced. And, the next season we won our conference championship and were very successful."

Always a Competition
"I never felt included by my teammates. It was a really cutthroat environment, and so you would make your few close friends, and then the rest were just there. I think our coach wanted it like that. It was always a competition so everyone was competing with each other. I remember hearing girls complain, and wish another teammate would mess up or get injured so that they could get into the game. Girls actually wished injuries on their own teammates! It was unbelievable to me."

Split Team
"There was just a lot of negative competition between my teammates, and no one wanted to support each other. It was really weird, and different than high school. And it got to be the worst during my junior year. There were three seniors on the team. They went to the coach one day and told him that the team had voted them captains, but we had never voted. They would tell him that the team decided on certain things, but we had actually never decided on it. And then they would always tattle on our teammates. They basically made it a split team. And then the coach wouldn't believe that they were doing these horrible things and were making these decisions. So it was just really nasty."

Team Chemistry -- So Good
"My freshman year was really tough, and the reason I stuck it out was because of my teammates. I felt really unprepared physically for the experience of Division 1. I really didn't want to go through it, but because the team chemistry was so good, and I had an amazing roommate, I stuck it out. Having really great teammates surrounding me made it much easier to stick around."

Really Close

"Our team is pretty close. There are little groups where certain ones hang out more often with others. Usually it's by grade. But when it comes to being on the field and in the locker room, everyone is social with everyone. We do a lot of things together outside of soccer too, such as team dinners, movies and nights out. We most always spend our weekend nights together as a whole team."

Supportive and Kind

"My teammates had an East Coast vibe, so they were not as huggy or Minnesota Nice as I was used to, but they were super nice in their own way. They would do things to make you feel included. For example, three of us had knee surgery in the spring and when we got back from our rehab, our teammates had left huge baskets of cookies, brownies, and protein bars and a note signed by everyone on our beds."

Best Friends

"My teammates have 100% always been my best friends. It's not even best friends, it's like family and sisters. I say sisters because we fight and we bicker and get at each other's throats, but they're the people who are there to tackle you onto the ground after you make a PK, they're the people who are there when you are crying or laughing. There's no filter together whatsoever. You are around each other 24/7. You become a family. We come from all over the country. It's insane, because everyone comes from completely different backgrounds and completely different families. It's crazy how one common goal can bring a team together."

Help Each Other Thrive

"Our team atmosphere is really great. I think each and every person knows when to be serious, and when it's time to let loose. We all support one another. We pick each other up when someone is down, and help him or her thrive even more when they are on a high."

Roller Coaster

"On our team, the highs are high, and the lows are low. It is a roller coaster every single day with our head coach. I think our assistant coaches would even agree that you don't really know what to expect from our coach on any given day. We like to think our coach does not dictate our attitude, but at the end of the day, it truly is dictated by the mood of our coach. In every single team huddle we remind each other that it is not how the coach says it, but what he says, that is important. This means that you can't worry if he swears at you or yells in your face. Just listen to what he says."

Respectful and Close
"I was close with everyone. I felt like I got along with pretty much everyone. Of course, there are always teammates you may not prefer to hang out with, but they are your teammates so you respect them. I had a level of respect for people and other people had a level of respect for me. With that being said, I think there are parts of the team that are very cliquey and kind of exclusive. I didn't want to be a part of those groups, but I think that played a role in how the team chemistry was."

Competition Made Us Better
"I think naturally everyone is very, very competitive, including myself. It makes everyone better; at least that's how I view it. I think it's super necessary. I'd be lying if I never felt competitive against another player that was trying to take my spot. At the same time I was thankful that they were there, because I knew they were pushing me."

Close-knit Family
"I absolutely loved my team for all four years. Of course, there was drama here and there, but that happens on every team. It was a very close-knit, family type of team. The things that I will remember forever are the bus and plane rides. The times spent with my teammates in ordinary places are what I'll remember forever."

Brotherhood
"My team is definitely a brotherhood. I guess the easiest way to describe my team is it's like a fraternity. You don't have time for much else, or to join other fraternities, so essentially, it becomes our own football fraternity. We usually hang out together, do everything together, since we spend a majority of our day together, so it's only natural that those guys become the people who you hang out with, and who you spend your time with."

Competition Made Us Better
"We are all super competitive. We all run together really well, and we work together really well, so that really helps us when it comes to our events because we all keep each other motivated and doing our best."

Things to Consider When You Meet A Prospective Team:

- Is competition fueling negative energy or positive support?
- How do they interact during practice and/or competition?
- What are they saying about each other?
- Does the atmosphere feel comfortable to you?
- Do the athletes enjoy each other outside the sport? What do they do together?
- Do the athletes have friends outside sport?
- Where do you want to find your next group of friends?
- How motivated are you for constant competition?

Stories about Life Beyond Sports
Insights into the social and extracurricular life of D1 athletes

No Off-Season
"As a Division I athlete, even in the off-season there is no off-season. As a Division I athlete, there is no studying abroad, there is no joining Greek life, there is no freedom to call your own. Now, when you look at NCAA Division I for what it is, a business, it makes sense. You, the athlete, are an investment, they pay you to perform and in return you do exactly as they say for a free or reduced education and degree. Now, if this outlook is bothersome, rethink what you want out of college."

Social Media Disappointments
"My freshman year was really difficult to adjust to being a student athlete because I just wanted to meet everyone, and do things, and have fun—and then social media sucks because you see everyone doing these fun things and you think you can too, but in reality you can't because you don't have the time. And sometimes you just really don't have any energy."

Sacrifice Is Worth It
"During the school week I'm usually really tired, so I don't really do much besides school and soccer. Occasionally (maybe once or twice a month), I'll go out of my way to hang out with people from my school and play video games or go out to eat with them but that's about it. On weekends, besides game days, I usually go out to parties or the bars now that I'm 21. I would say, though, I miss out on a lot, and you do have to sacrifice lots of time. You can't go out as much as you would like. I've also missed a lot of fun events like concerts or random things, because I have to worry about soccer. I feel the sacrifice is worth it."

Hanging Out with Fellow Athletes
"I definitely had some close friends outside of the football team and the athletic program. But, I certainly didn't have the chance to participate a lot with people outside of the athletic department, because all of my time was spent there. I found myself hanging out with my fellow athletes."

Not as Involved as High School
"I was involved in a lot of things in high school, like Student Government. I tried to do it in college, but it was so hard. Every time we had a meeting, I had practice. You can't really be involved in things outside of your sport, like you could be in high school. I was a president of Student Government in high school, but in college, I was barely a

member. You have to pick and choose what you really want to focus on, because you don't really have the time to do it all (or the need or the desire). That goes for friendships too. In college you make really great friendships, but it's not like high school where you are friends with tons of different people."

Sports Crowd
"In college, I hang out with more people who play sports than I did in high school. In high school, I would spend time with people who did and did not play sports. In college I feel like my main base of friends are people who play sports."

Reel It In and Control It
"Certain people can handle certain limits to their social life. In high school, as soon as I found running and realized that I was pretty good it, I was okay with sacrificing my social life for running. Like not going out on a Friday night, or not going to the dance on a Thursday, or not going out to see friends on certain days. You'd miss out on certain things to make sure you were prepared for the next practice or the next meet. I was used to that. I was used to sacrificing. I think that made me ready for college athletically, because it is all about sacrifice. It's all about delayed gratification, because maybe you don't get gratified until the last meet of the season. If you are able to do that, then you are going to be a stronger athlete. Once you get to college, you are forced to give up a social life or at least reel it in and control it. Looking back as a graduate, I think sometimes I do regret being so comfortable with letting that go."

I Wish I Had More Non-Athlete Friends
"My freshman year I had a non-athlete roommate, which was really nice. It forced me to branch out. I wish that I had more non-athlete friends. I think I always felt that way. Athlete friends are great and they're cool people, but I think they tend to isolate. They stay with their team. I think whenever that happens it turns into an in-group thing where they don't really respect other groups or other students. I hated that. That really alienated me, and I really didn't like that at all."

Learned to Balance it All
"Although I do not have too many friends outside of my team or even the athletic department, I do have a really great network of friends who support what I do, and I still get to spend a significant amount of time with. While being a student-athlete, I was able to fall in love with someone, have time to date him, and am now currently engaged to him! It is hard to maintain a full social life, but I think once you master how to balance everything, all aspects of your life fall into place."

Social Got Kicked to the Curb
"If you ask me to name people outside of the athletic center I really don't know many. My parents always say that you can succeed at two things at the same time, but when you bring a third into the mix, it is hard. In this situation, it would be school, sport and social. School and sport were my main priorities, and social kind of got kicked to the curb. Any social time I did have was spent with my teammates."

Very Active Social Life
"I think I had a very good social life considering that I was an athlete. I went out frequently and did a lot in the city. I can't say it was as active as a non-athlete student, but I can't really complain. I loved going to museums in the city."

Joined the Club
"My social life was good. I joined a fraternity and I was in an eating club, which is unique to my school. But it's where all the social life is centered. Fraternities are like the underground things. The eating clubs are like the big things."

Sorority and Study Abroad
"I was in a sorority, but I still was not able to do a lot of stuff because of the team. The main reason I actually chose my university was because it was the only DI school that I could find that had an opening for my position in volleyball, and gave me the opportunity to study abroad. That was something I had to do in college. I just knew that was something that was really important to me. And so that was the coolest thing I was able to do outside of school and volleyball. We had January term to do traveling trips, so I did a bunch of those, and I also did a semester abroad, which was my biggest thing outside of school and volleyball."

Unpleasant
"Social Life? There wasn't one. Girls would tattle on my team if anyone went out socially. The fear of getting in trouble/tattled on made the team culture a very unpleasant one."

Nothing Allowed Beyond Sports
"My two best friends were a volleyball player and a soccer player. I spent a lot of time with one boy in my Spanish class because he always helped me catch up on the work I missed with soccer. I really did not have any time to socialize. We could not participate in any clubs or activities, or any sororities. My coach did not even allow us to participate in freshman orientation so I never really got to meet anyone in my class or be part of any of the welcome festivities."

Things to Investigate about Life Beyond Sports:

- How does the coach describe how the team socializes?
- How does the coach describe what is allowed beyond sports? What examples are provided?

- How do your potential teammates describe life outside of sport?
- Ask specifically what they are involved in:
    - How do they spend weekends without competition?
    - Can they join clubs or Greek life?
    - Can they study abroad?
    - What is the off-season like?
    - What is the summer like?

Be sure to get a complete picture from as many individuals as possible to compare similarities and differences as you investigate your options.

For Your Consideration ...

Your thoughts about their stories?
　　What matches your hopes?
　　What surprises you?
　　… What will work for you?

Worksheet: What Do I Really Want in College?

The following statements provide a sampling of the wide range of opportunities in college. Rate each statement with the following scale:

0 = not important; **1** = might be important; **2** = definitely important; **3** = extremely important

Assessment Statements	A	B	C	D
In college, it is important to me that I...				
Find friends who will be in my life forever				
Maintain high standards academically				
Gain work experience in preparation for my career				
Be recognized as a standout athlete				
In college, I want to be able to ...				
Go out with my friends regularly				
Choose the classes that I want to take				
Participate in clubs/activities to develop myself				
Hang out with all types of athletes				
On a typical weekday, I want to...				
Have time to go eat or study with friends				
Have enough time to study and prepare for class				
Have time to relax and watch TV				
Get in an extra workout session in the gym				

I definitely want to experience…		
Traveling and exploring with friends		
Traveling abroad		
A summer internship related to future goals		
Traveling for my sport		
Ideally, I would…		
Have a boyfriend/girlfriend		
Maintain high grades		
Participate actively on campus		
Be recognized on campus for my athletic success		
It would make me really happy to…		
Find a great group of friends who hang out regularly		
Major in something that I am passionate about		
Hold a leadership role on campus		
Set records in my sport		
I definitely want to take advantage of …		
Spring break trips with my friends		
Traveling abroad for a semester		
My dream internship		
Training trips with my team		

When I imagine college, I see myself...		
Surrounded by friends who will be in my life always		
Excelling in the classroom		
Becoming prepared to 'stand-out' in my career		
As an athlete with a great team		
In college, I want to...		
Have time to relax and hang out with my friends		
Do well at school		
Eat healthy		
Do weekend activities with my teammates		
On Friday and Saturdays, I want to be able to...		
Go to themed parties with friends		
Study with friends in the library		
Attend school wide tailgates		
Compete in my sport		
I prefer to....		
Study with my friends regularly		
Study by myself in a café or library		
Relax and study at the same time		
Study in mandatory athlete study-hall sessions		

I will happily attend...				
Social events with my friends				
Lectures from professionals in my area of study				
Campus wide events (tailgates, speakers, etc.)				
Weekend/late night practices				

Total Score Per Column				
	A	B	C	D

Each column represents a preference towards a grouping of activities. The higher the score in the column, the stronger your preferences for those activities.

> **Column A** is a preference for social activities, including things like studying with friends, Greek life, club participation, spring break trips, themed parties, dances, and more.
>
> **Column B** indicates a high commitment to quality academics, and freedom to study in ways that are comfortable to you.
>
> **Column C** indicates a desire to gain personal and professional readiness opportunities.
>
> **Column D** confirms your commitment and strong focus on athletics.

You can be high in all columns, or just a few. Your preferences show you how to evaluate the priorities and allowances of the coaches/programs you are considering. Be sure to question the coach and team to confirm that you can participate in the activities that you ranked important or extremely important on this worksheet.

What did I learn from this assessment?

Worksheet: Focus on Four!

Overview: Getting what you want out of any experience means knowing what you're hoping for. In this exercise you need to choose four descriptive phrases that clarify what will make this the best and most rewarding college experience you can imagine. Several word choices are listed below. The words that have been "lined out" (~~lined out~~) cannot be included in your chart. They are over-used, unclear, catchall words. You need to take time and be honest and clear about what you want in each facet of your upcoming college and athletic experience.

Instructions: Circle the phrases that best describe the experience you hope to have in each category. Then map the words to the FACETS CHART on the following page. Feel free to add in additional descriptive words of your choice. This is about you being honest and clear about what will make you happy in your college and athletic experience.

Interpretation: Keep your Facets Chart in mind as you consider each potential college option. Make sure that the experience you hope for matches the experience you sign up for.

Coach	Team	Social Life
<ul><li>funny</li><li>serious</li><li>personal</li><li>strict</li><li>creative</li><li>friend like</li><li>famous</li></ul>	<ul><li>big group</li><li>small group</li><li>~~friendly~~</li><li>competitive</li><li>supportive</li><li>~~inclusive~~</li><li>closely bonded</li></ul>	<ul><li>party often</li><li>party never</li><li>activities off campus</li><li>eating with friends</li><li>bars and clubs</li><li>lazy mornings</li></ul>
Academics	Experiences	Life Style
<ul><li>~~high quality~~</li><li>~~selective~~</li><li>take my major</li><li>great teachers</li><li>independent study</li><li>internship</li><li>research projects</li><li>class discussions</li><li>online course</li></ul>	<ul><li>~~exciting~~</li><li>internship</li><li>clubs</li><li>Greek life</li><li>Student Govt.</li><li>~~fun~~</li><li>study abroad</li><li>fund raising</li><li>social service</li></ul>	<ul><li>spontaneous</li><li>explore new places</li><li>try new things</li><li>meet new people</li><li>travel</li><li>activities off campus</li><li>work / intern</li></ul>

Focus on Four!

Add four words that best describe what you hope to experience in each of the following facets of your college and athletic life. Remember these words during your visits. Check if these words accurately match the programs you are considering.

Focus on Four		
Coach	**Team**	**Social Life**
Academics	**Experiences**	**Life Style**

Worksheet: What Do I Really Want in a Coach?

The following statements provide a sampling of the wide range of relationship qualities of college coaches. Rate each statement with the following scale:

0 = not important; **1** = might be important; **2** = definitely important; **3** = extremely important

Assessment Statements	A	B	C
The best coaches...			
Encourage unity, hard work, and sportsmanship			
Structure practice in engaging and creative ways			
Have excellent competition tactics and skills to win			
A good coach...			
Leads by example; sets high standards and models it			
Is enthusiastic about training and competition			
Focuses on teaching skills key to winning			
I would like people to say that my coach...			
Brought the best out of me as an athlete and person			
Treated athletes with respect			
Was a winning coach			
I would like my relationship with my coach to be...			
He/she knows me well as a person			
He/she is supportive when I need it			
He/she focuses strictly on how I can excel as an athlete			

In practice, I want my coach to be...			
Teaching skills that can be used throughout life			
Flexible and creative in devising ways to achieve performance goals			
Doing whatever necessary to produce winners			
I would like my coach to communicate with me...			
Regularly, and provide constructive feedback			
Ways in which I can improve as an athlete			
Tactics to produce wins			
Total Score Per Column			
	A	B	C

Each column represents a preference towards priorities that you value from your coach. The higher your score in the column, the stronger your preferences for that perspective.

Column A shows a preference for a focus on athlete development

Column B indicates a high commitment for a healthy environment

Column C shows a strong preference to win

You can be high in all columns, or just a few. Your preferences show you how to evaluate the priorities and practices of the coaches/programs you are considering. Be sure to question the coach and team to confirm that your preferences match the coaching climate at each college you explore.

What did I learn from this assessment?

> *"It was the best of times, it was the worst of times, it was the age of wisdom, it was the age of foolishness, it was the epoch of belief, it was the epoch of incredulity ... we had everything before us, we had nothing before us ... "*
>
> -Charles Dickens, *A Tale of Two Cities*

4
Know the Risks

Participating in D1 athletics is not easy. It's a challenge beyond anything most high school athletes have encountered. You might be ready – but the truth is, you hardly know what to expect.

The commitment to D1 most often means athletic training with more discipline and rigor than ever before. Competition is more intense, and creates a deep ripple effect into team dynamics, especially when athletics is tied to money in ticket/media revenues, or more personally in scholarship funds. It's a context of extreme discipline and sacrifice in which almost every decision is based on athletics.

Of course, there are tremendous variations across programs based on the administrators and coaching staff, team dynamics, expectations and climate. You need to look for signs that the programs in your selection pool align with your goals for college and your values for living. The recruiting process is your time to think broadly and make a thoughtful, informed personal choice. It's about YOU living YOUR DREAM, whatever you determine that to be.

This section includes anecdotes based on our interviews with D1 athletes. We asked each athlete, "What was your worst experience?" – and they provided a range of responses. We are not saying or implying that any of these scenarios will happen to everyone, or even happen to you. But, perhaps like you, the athletes we interviewed never expected to find themselves in the midst of these challenges. Use their stories to help you have a realistic perspective on what could go wrong, so you can listen and observe more closely during your recruiting visits. Accept this opportunity with your eyes wide open, and make your D1 commitment from an informed perspective that will provide a solid foundation for success going forward.

Before you read their stories,
What difficulties have your friends experienced in college athletics?

Stories about Harsh Realities
Insights from D1 athletes about their worst experiences

Team Hierarchies
"One practice, when I was an underclassman, I was going head to head with one of the senior girls who was the starter in my position. I was doing really well in practice against her, and in one drill, I beat her. She got frustrated that I won, and so she two hand shoved me to the ground in front of my coach. Nothing was addressed. Being an underclassman, and being at the bottom of the social hierarchy on the team, and then having my coach witness me being shoved to the ground with her own two eyes and turning her head just didn't sit well with me. It sucks because there is a social hierarchy on the team made up of what class you are in and how much you play, which is hard because I don't want to be looked down upon when I am trying to learn, and do my best. You just don't feel respected."

Team Dynamics
"My worst experiences with D1 athletics have been dealing with the players on my team. Most of us do not get along. We rarely get though a practice without one teammate getting in a verbal altercation with another. The same is true for the time we are forced to spend together off the court. What makes it so bad is how basketball is so time consuming so we're around each other everyday, all year round."

Not Enough Hours in the Day
"The worst memories of playing a sport in college are when you feel that you do not have enough hours in the day. For example, this week I have three exams, and am forced to spend every free moment studying. It's difficult to be disciplined every moment of the day, to plan out how I can strategically get all my work done and still get enough sleep to perform well in practice or games. It is absolutely exhausting, and it can be difficult to remember why I am doing this to myself."

You Can Be Replaced
"The competition is harder. Coaches care less about you in college because you can be replaced."

Tough Transition to Start
"My worst memories and experiences of my Division 1 athletic experience involve the transition into college, which is something that I believe most students have to go through. My second semester was very difficult coming back from Christmas break,

and I had to talk with a lot of people to get through the hard time. Also, our team atmosphere did not start off very well. I expected to come into college and have immediate best friends, but that was definitely not the case. I actually dreaded practice and play for quite a while. It has improved some now."

Scholarship Expectations
"My worst memories are how I was treated. Because I was on such a large scholarship, I was pretty much on the payroll, and my coaches never let me forget that. I was treated much differently than my roommate who was not on scholarship. Nothing was ever good enough. I felt like I had the scholarship dollar amount written on my back. That was all my coaches saw."

Internal Competition
"I was recruited to this school based on how the team was a family, and how they would treat me with respect and not play games with me like my high school coach did. None of this ended up being true. In D1 sports, it is so competitive that it is very hard to have a family. Everyone is competing against each other for those precious travel spots. Your teammates seem to be okay with you failing as long as they themselves succeed."

Coach Departure
"My worst memory of my Division 1 athletic experience was when, only a few months into my first semester, our coach informed the team she would be leaving. As a freshman who was just getting adjusted to my university, this came as a shock and honestly, I did not know what to do. I had chosen the school mainly for the coach, which meant I had to reconsider my decision of even coming to this school in the first place, and decide whether I wanted to transfer or not."

Going Without Sleep
"My worst memories are not doing well in class and always being tired. There is no doubt that in season you will have to sacrifice. Sometimes that goes further than extracurricular activities. Sometimes that means sleep is sacrificed and one night of terrible sleep can lead to a whole week of being tired. Football is a little different than some sports because it is ALWAYS high intensity, and if you don't schedule properly, you will find yourself tired, always sore, and doing poorly academically because you cannot stay awake. You will have to sacrifice and plan if you want to be the best student and ball player possible."

Self-Induced Stress
"My worst experience is the stress soccer puts on me. I want to be a player who contributes, and who is on the field, so I am always pushing myself to the next level. When I make mistakes, I am thinking about how this will affect my playing time or if I will be taken off the field. It is very competitive within the team, and this competitiveness is something that drives me, but it also stresses me out."

Missing Out on School Activities
"Another downside being an athlete is that I feel that I cannot take advantage of school activities that regular students partake in because my schedule does not permit it. There are events, clubs, and meetings that my major promotes you to join or go to, but due to my busy schedule, these things can't be fit in. Therefore, I feel that I am missing out on that."

No Guarantees
"The initial coach that recruited me got fired my senior year of high school. This was a disappointment because he was the main reason why I chose the school. He was laid back and let the girls have lives outside of soccer, and school always came first which I liked. Once the new coach was hired I had a positive outlook and thought things would all workout. I went and visited the spring of my senior year and things went okay. I was confident as an incoming freshman. I got to preseason and had trouble with the fitness test (which really sucked because I trained all summer and felt confident in my endurance). I took the test multiple times before passing. My coach wouldn't even let me and others even touch a soccer ball before we passed. We ran and ran until we couldn't run anymore. I felt like I was on a cross country or track team. I spent the majority of my preseason and freshman year on the school track rather than a soccer field (this was not what I signed up for). Once I finally had permission to practice I was never involved in the team play, always a sideline passer, or shagged balls during shooting drills etc. Then, games came around. I was not even allowed to wear my jersey while sitting on the bench. It was unreal. I had never felt so NOT part of a team in my life. My coach's rules and the way she treated the lower tier players (mostly freshman whom she had not recruited) was just cruel. I was so depressed. I hated soccer. There wasn't a day I wanted to go to bed because I knew I would have to wake up in the morning and go to practice."

Injury Changes Everything
"My worst memory happened my senior year. In the second game, I dislocated my ankle. That was definitely tough to cope with. I was able to come back towards the end of the year. Unfortunately, I wasn't able to come back in a role that was the same before the injury. My ankle just wasn't able to come back to where I could contribute as a starter. Dealing with the adversity, and knowing that it was my senior year and

that it happened on a cheap play during my first collegiate start, was awful. It was definitely difficult to deal with, but it made me a stronger person moving forward. I'll be able to fight through a lot of things moving forward."

Deflated On the Bench
"The most painful experiences came from not being able to play in the games. That was heart breaking because of how much I would put into it. I would get such huge anxiety on the sidelines wondering if I would get in and thinking that if I got in, I needed to do everything perfectly so that I could stay in. I'm someone who is very hard on myself, so it can be very draining mentally and very painful emotionally. Even in my fifth year, when I was playing a lot, and then got injured, I would again be sitting on the bench. It never got easy to be the player on the bench."

Bullying
"I was bullied at the end of my sophomore year. I left a volunteer thing early, because we had a ton of extra volunteers. I had asked the people in charge of the volunteering event if they minded if I left two hours early, because my boyfriend flew in to surprise me. They didn't mind at all, because they said they had too many volunteers. The next day, three of my teammates went to my coach to tell him that I left early. He suspended me for three days, because I left early. It just catapulted from there, because then I didn't trust my teammates. I was wondering what was the point of that. They could've just talked to me personally. There was no need to bring in coach, but they didn't seem to get that. They just wanted to see me fail."

No Reality; No Control
"Once my original assistant coach left my sophomore year, the dynamics totally switched. My head coach was no longer the nice and understanding person he used to be. He just became very judgmental and very abrasive. After every practice the majority of players would wonder what his problem was. For some individuals it was worse. For me, if I would get hurt during two-a-days, he would tell me that I was actually hurt from the summer when I was doing stuff that I never actually did. It was really bad. He would make me sit out of games for past injuries, not even injuries that I had at that moment. He would hold grudges from me being hurt. That was an issue."

Why Not Me?
"This is more of a personal experience. We have lost six people from my class. We started with nine and went to seven after freshman year. We are now down to three going into our senior year. That right there shows you my coach's style. People quit because they realized that what they were being told wasn't actually going to happen. Like I said, now we are down to three of us in the senior class. We voted for captains, but she didn't really say anything. She just told us to write down who we wanted to be

captain. She chose two out of the three of us. I was the one not chosen. It is perfectly fine, but I took that as a very personal dig, as she went out of her way to not make me a captain. There were only three of us and she just didn't choose me. I took it really hard. I took it a lot more personally than I probably needed to. That was a really tough moment for me."

Feeling Worthless
"My difficult memories stem from the fact that Division 1 athletics is not as much of a community as I thought it was. A lot of times it seems like our coaching staff and our teams are separate entities. What I mean is if I wasn't running good enough times to put me in the big conference races, then I would receive a lot less attention and coaching. My biggest example of this is after one race when a teammate and I didn't perform our best, we went up to our coach and he said something like, 'I'm not even sure why I coach middle distance athletes, because they have no heart. You guys don't have heart.' He had a philosophy that if athletes are not running good times, then they must not care, or they must not be dedicated enough, or they have no value. Those kinds of moments were very eye-opening for me, and alienating, and isolating honestly. It was infuriating to hear my coach say that."

Verbal Abuse
"My coach is not afraid to verbally curse you out. During the recruiting process, my dad asked if he would be able to watch practice. Coach just looked at him and said – 'no.' It became clear that you couldn't watch practice. That was a red flag. Like why did he say no so quickly? Honestly, I don't think anyone wants to visit practice, because then they would feel obligated to share their story about what they heard on the field. You have this cycle where everyone will say that we have this great coach, but no one will actually watch our practice because then they'll feel obligated to report him. It makes no sense."

Emotional Abuse
"When I think of bad memories I think of my coaches. At my first school, I had a coach who kept harping on my fitness. She would make me do fitness on off days when everyone else was resting. There was a time when we had just gotten a new assistant coach, and she came to the fitness center, and she personally pressed the buttons on the treadmill I was running on. I will remember this forever, because I was at the point of breaking down. I got off the treadmill, and she looked at me, and she was like 'why are you doing this?' And I asked what she meant. She said, 'you are wasting your time, you are wasting my time, you are wasting your teammates time,' then she said, 'Do you even want to play D1, because honestly I don't think you're going to make it.' She said that I should really consider going D2. At that point, I got off the treadmill and walked away. I saw my best friend and teammate and she saw me crying. I told her what happened, and then I asked myself if I wanted to continue doing this."

Disgusting Disrespect
"My coach bullied me. One time my coach kicked me out of practice, because I messed up. When I mess up I literally yell at myself. I messed up this drill like three times in a row and she told us to stop. I was so frustrated and so I tried to relax. Then she's like, 'just go home.' I looked at her confused, and she's like, 'did you not hear what I said? Grab your sh*t and go the f*ck home.' I still thought she was kidding, and then she's like, 'do you understand? Grab your sh*t and go the f*ck home.' So I just left and sat in the locker room for a couple hours and waited for them to get out of practice."

Crushing
"I tried to have a talk with my coach at the end of my sophomore year. I am not one for confrontation. I really planned out what to say because I was really nervous. I knew if I didn't speak up, I wouldn't forgive myself for not trying. I asked if I was ever going to be good enough to play on the team. And coach said, 'probably not.' That was a really hard experience. It made me not want to go anywhere. It hurt, and then it stung. I'm still here though."

Psychological Games
"The whole year my coach would just bully me and never give me a chance. Coach would let me practice, and then would travel me for big trips, but would never let me play in games. And then for other trips, coach would keep me back and make me do these extra workouts that were crazy intense. I passed out during two or three of them. And, there was no reason to be doing everything to me."

Inappropriateness
"My worst memory was a time when a lifting coach made a really ridiculously inappropriate comment to me, and it wasn't the only time that he did it to me, or other girls on the team. I went to the administration, and said something to them about what he had said to me, and the administration backed me up about it and was there for me about it. But then when it came to my coach, he called this whole meeting with the team and basically stood up for the lifting coach and not me. Coach said the most inappropriate things to me, and I was like really, is this what you would say to your daughter? You wouldn't help her, or support her when a guy said something about her ass in front of everyone! It was just completely inappropriate. He was a nasty coach."

Lack of Concern
"One day during fitness practice the whole team was running timed miles. One of the older girls fainted on the track right in front of me. I stopped, like anyone would do, to try and help her, make sure she was okay. She fell hard and could have really hit her head hard. And, everyone was so tired and fatigued; I was worried someone was going to trip or step on her and hurt her. I bent down to see if she was okay and my coach

screamed at me, 'leave her, finish your mile,' and then she yelled at the trainers, 'get her off the track NOW.' There was no sense of concern in her voice. My coach actually sounded annoyed that my teammate was blocking the track, as if she had purposely fainted to ruin the drill."

Never Good Enough
"I was never good enough for my coach, my boss, and the man who brought me here and is paying me to perform. My head coach was never satisfied with my performance. The four shutouts I helped produce, the undefeated and shutout tournament championship did not seem to be enough. Finishing first in sprints, showing some of the largest improvements in the weight room, there was always something that was not good enough. And because of this daily, passive-aggressive, nagging, I fell out of love with the sport that had stolen my heart as a child."

Things to Consider During Your Visit:

- Ask the coach about the toughest challenges for past athletes.
- Ask the coach about the transfer rate. How many athletes leave each year?
- What happens when you're not on the travel squad?
- Ask for a description of athletes who were injured in the past couple of seasons.
- Do you feel competition between the athletes?
- How will you feel about the program if the coach leaves?
- Are you ready to face the possibility of being replaced in any year?
- Do the athletes have any issues with the program? What are their challenges?
- If you asked the athletes for their worst experiences, what would they say? Can you live with similar experiences?

Plan for the Worst:

- Where is the local hospital? Is it good enough? What other medical resources can be used if necessary?
- What is your back up plan if you accept this opportunity and it doesn't work out?

For Your Consideration ...

Your thoughts about their stories?
What matches your thoughts?
What surprises you?
… What will work for you?

Worksheet: Are You Prepared for the Worst?

Overview: We all know that college athletics will put you in demanding, rigorous, stressful situations. Our interviews with D1 athletes illustrate both the best and worst of times. While we hope for the best, we need to prepare for the worst. So, as you think about achieving your spot in college athletics, take some time to reflect on how you will handle the challenges these athletes faced.

- How can you be strong if these occur in your first weeks?
- What are your strategies for personal support?
- How can your family help, until your friends and teammates are established?
- Would you be willing to use counselors for support and for your personal well-being if needed?

Instructions: Review the challenges that our interviewees described in their worst experiences. Determine how you might feel in each situation, and then anticipate how you could best support yourself in similar circumstances. Thinking about this in advance will make you stronger in your upcoming college experience.

Potential Challenges	My Strategy to Handle This
- Competitive Teammates (not friends)	
- Broken Promises	
- Team Politics	
- Not Enough Hours in the Day	
- Feeling that You Can Be Replaced	
- Tough Transition Getting Started	
- Feeling Sore and Worn Out	
- Scholarship Expectations	
- Coach Departure	
- Going Without Sleep	
- Uncontrollable Feelings of Stress	

▪ Missing Out on School Activities	
▪ Overtraining Beyond Exhaustion	
▪ Sidelined with No Options	
▪ Injury that Changes Everything	
▪ Deflated On the Bench	
▪ Feeling Bullied By Teammates/Coach	
▪ Why Not Me? Why Can't I Play?	
▪ Made to Feel Worthless	
▪ Verbal Abuse	
▪ Emotional Abuse	
▪ Deep Disrespect	
▪ Crushed by Coach Feedback	
▪ Sexual Inappropriateness	
▪ Feeling Not Good Enough	
What other challenges do you think about?	

> *"Education helps us be better people. It helps us be better citizens. You came to college to learn about the world and to engage with new ideas and to discover the things you're passionate about -- and maybe have a little fun. And to expand your horizons. That's terrific -- that's a huge part of what college has to offer.*
>
> *But you're also here, now more than ever, because a college degree is the surest ticket to the middle class. It is the key to getting a good job that pays a good income -- and to provide you the security where even if you don't have the same job for 30 years, you're so adaptable and you have a skill set and the capacity to learn new skills, it ensures you're always employable.*
>
> *And that is the key not just for individual Americans, that's the key for this whole country's ability to compete in the global economy. In the new economy, jobs and businesses will go wherever the most skilled, best-educated workforce resides... And I want them to look no further than the United States of America."*
>
> -Barack Obama, JD, 44th President of the United States
>
> Given in remarks at Pellissippi State Community College; Tennessee, Jan. 9, 2015, available at www.whitehouse.gov

5
Academic Practicalities

Let's be frank. The purpose of college is your preparation and readiness for the world of work. As you explore various recruiting opportunities, you need to investigate the realities and practicalities of your academic preparation. You and only you need to make sure that college will lay the foundation that you need to get a good job and create a happy, fulfilling life.

Optimizing academics while being a good athlete is really hard. One key to success is finding an athletic program that truly values your academic success, as much as your performance. Administrators and coaches either promote "school first, athletics second" or "athletics first." This is a cultural phenomenon that is inherent in the program, and you would be best served to find a program that operates with the perspective you value. Don't leave this issue to chance. Perhaps the best way to figure this out is by asking the current athletes and their families, and listening to their experiences to inform your perspective and decision.

Based on our interviews with D1 athletes, let's take a look at what they have experienced, as a way to help you more clearly articulate what you are hoping for, and what you can manage, in balancing college athletics and academics.

Before you read their stories,
What are your hopes for college academics?

Stories about Academics

Insights from D1 athletes about academics, professors, and professional opportunities

In this section, the stories have been grouped by common themes, to help clarify some of the major considerations in balancing both athletics and academics. The sections included are as follows:

- Academic Advisor Support (a special privilege of D1 programs)
- Working with Professors
- Balancing Academics and Athletics
- A Few Things Missed
- Long Term Tradeoffs

As throughout the book, the stories remain in the original words of the athletes.

-- Academic Advisor Support --

Inside Track
"I have an athletic advisor who helps me set up my classes. He actually has my class schedule decided once I declare my major, so then we just use that to sign up for courses each semester. That's how I get the right courses. Also, my academic advisor tries to set me up with teachers that he knows work well with athletes. All the academic advisors know the teachers that will be helpful when you have to miss class for away games and things like that."

Scheduling Privileges
"I haven't really found any negatives of being a student-athlete because we get to select our schedule before everyone else. We can tailor it around our practices and meets. I found it actually a little bit easier to transition from high school to college. There is so much more free time in college."

Resources
"Being at a Division 1 program there are just so many resources at your fingertips. I'm speaking about my conference, because that's the one I am in. I know that for my conference, it's pretty standard across the board. There are just so many academic resources at your disposal. I had an academic advisor who I'd meet with every week, and she would help me with a plan to make sure I was getting all my schoolwork done. Then a month before the next semester, she would start discussing what classes I would need to take the following semester. She made sure I was on top of everything."

Multi-faceted Support
"The sole job of our academic advising team is to make sure that we graduate on time, and that our classes don't interfere with practice times. Our graduate assistant has made sure that we are on track with our current classes. I've sat down with him for hours to talk about not having the energy to go do homework after playing. I just don't have the motivation to go to the library sometimes."

Broad Support
"We are all assigned to one academic advisor. Each sport has one. Whenever I have problems with my professors, or if I don't like my classes, I can go to him and he will help us. He does all of our scheduling, and picks out all of our classes for us. He pretty much does all of our classes and scheduling for us."

-- Working with Professors --

Fly Under the Radar
"Usually I try to fly under the radar as an athlete, unless I have to tell professors I'm leaving for a game or something. I know some teammates who feel that they get treated worse as athletes. Some teachers don't like athletes, or just don't like our sport. Some of the stories I have heard are ridiculous and are obviously cases of professors being out to get my teammates. But for me, I was usually treated equally."

Trouble with Travel
"We were instructed to give our professors our travel letters and schedules the first day of class. We could tell right away what professors were going to be nice or not. If they were rude -- we would switch out of their class right away."

Some Stereotypes
"There are some professors that will look at you and judge you because you are an athlete. They immediately assume that you are going to slack off. I've never had a professor be like, oh my god you're an athlete, in a positive way. In fact, it's always more of a negative thing like, oh you're not going to turn in your homework and oh you're going to miss class all the time. You have to work against the stereotype. Professors don't believe that school is a first priority for athletes, but that's not true."

Empathy and Tolerance
"My professors typically gave me a lot of slack as an athlete. I remember my statistics professor. I had his sports statistics class every morning at 10:30 right after I got out of practice and my lifts. I would eat breakfast in his class because I never had time to do

so beforehand. Many days, I would even fall asleep, only to be woken up at the end of class by him. He never got mad, just handed me all the handouts and made sure I wrote down the homework. I remember feeling really guilty and ashamed. I was a great student in high school. Sleeping in class is not who I am. But I was so exhausted. It was nice that he understood and didn't yell at me. I honestly think he felt badly for me. I think I only didn't get into trouble because he knew I was on the soccer team, and soccer at my school was a big deal. I also ended up with an A in his class."

Compensating for Missing Class
"I think some of my professors did treat me differently because I was an athlete. For some reason, athletes have a reputation that you don't care about school as much, when that is not always the case. I think that as an athlete it is important to give each professor your travel letter after you introduce yourself, and then also let him or her know that you'll send an email before you leave to make sure you have the information to makeup any work that you miss. Also being really attentive in class will create less push back from your professors. I didn't receive much push back from my professors. There was one course that I ended up missing six classes for, and for every class I missed, I had to write two pages on an article, even though they were excused absences from the athletic department. She gave me all the points back. I would've gotten a C in the class if I hadn't made up the work."

It Helps to Participate and Care
"When I showed up to school, I was worried because I was in such a prestigious business school and I felt like my teachers would not want to deal with jocks. When I did my pre-requisite classes, the classes were so big that professors didn't even know my name. So they didn't know me to treat me differently. Once I got into my major classes, my junior and senior year, professors were awesome. All teachers want you to do is engage with them, or ask them questions. I learned that quickly, and always participated. Four other football guys were in my major and once a semester a professor would email coach raving about our participation in class. But we cared a lot about our education. Not all football guys are like that. A lot of football guys can get away with not going to class, or sitting on their laptops all day, because we can get away with that."

-- Balancing Academics and Athletics --

Finding a Way to Balance
"I was a transfer student, because academically, I was having trouble balancing everything at the first school that I went to. I was just so focused on soccer that I was neglecting to put that same amount of energy into my academics. Had I not transferred, I was thinking of doing a graduate program instead of trying to do pre-

med and soccer at the same time. I was considering just enjoying my sport and doing a really fun major like Art."

Enjoy Being Busy
"I never had any internships or jobs during school. I just had summer jobs when we had a month break just to keep myself busy. I know there were a few girls who had internships. I think there was one who was an intern at a law firm, so she had to juggle a busy schedule. She would be at practice, go to work, go to class, go back to work, and then go do homework. A lot of the girls who had jobs and internships were busy, but they always said that they enjoyed being busy. A lot of them were just busy bodies."

Can't Do It All
"As an Elementary Education major, I had to go see schools and do observations in schools, and I needed to spend time there as well. Elementary school is from 8am to 3:30pm, so that's usually a time I would've been busy at practice or something like that. That was a big part of my decision to leave. I knew that I could spend the time that I would usually be at practice, observing children and learning, and doing all these amazing things instead. There weren't any scheduling conflicts my first few years, but I knew there would've been in my junior and senior year, which is why I stopped running."

Focus on One Thing at a Time
"My academic experience does match what I hoped for in college. Sometimes, I do get a little less study time than I would like, or a little less time to perfect an assignment, but what I have always believed is that you will not be able to be perfect in all areas of life. I try to separate my days into academic, athletic and social events. When it is time for me to put on my athlete hat, I don't think about academics. When the academic hat goes on, athletics is not on my mind. And when I am being social, I am not thinking about either! It helps to give separation and my full attention to whatever part of my day I am at."

Easier Online
"In my undergrad I took some of my classes online. But all of my graduate classes are on campus. It was easier to take them online really. They were offered both in class and online, but with us traveling so much and training early, I figured it would be easier with my schedule to take them online."

Designate Time
"Academically, it is necessary to designate at least two hours a day to study and course work. Athletically, many hours of working out and practicing are required."

Missing 5-7 Days During Season
"In terms of missing actual class time, it didn't happen that often. Dual swim meets were on weekends, and it is pretty common for people to avoid Friday class, so that just subtracts a day that you miss. I probably missed more during the spring semester. In the spring I probably missed 5-7 days of class. With only 12-week semesters, missing a day can set you back a lot in your coursework."

It All Worked for Me
"I think I have been pretty lucky because I really have not run into issues scheduling classes and stuff, in terms of the ones I want to take. This semester I had the only class conflict with football ever. I study mechanical engineering, which is a lot more intense than typical degrees. When I came into the football program, they told me that it is hard to get classes to line up right without conflicts; it is almost expected that you will have class conflicts with practices times. But I have been fortunate that it has not happened to me more."

I Made it Work
"After my freshman year, my coach told me 'you know what, if you really want to play next year, you should stay on campus and train all summer.' So I was like, okay, and I did summer school on campus and played. It was the worst; it was so dumb. And then the next year, I didn't play. So I was like, screw this, I am never doing this again. And so then I decided to take different summer opportunities. We always had camps that we put on in July, so I basically just had the month of June for a summer. And so I did one month long internships every summer following my freshman year. These were hard to find, because no one wants someone just for a month, but it was good, it worked."

-- A Few Things Missed --

Hard to Be a Student First
"The emphasis here at my school is that you are a student athlete. But it is really hard to be a student first. It is really hard when you are traveling, when you are missing class, when you are dog tired for class at 10am because you had practice at 7am. It's hard when you are competing with other students who don't have that 20+ hours (per week) time commitment that I have. And I am still expected to perform at the same level in fear of being academically ineligible. So I want to say it doesn't matter, just because I am coached to say it doesn't matter. But it really does matter. It is the whole physical and mental tiredness of it. You can argue that regular students have 20 hour jobs a week, but my 20 hours are physical, emotional, and mental exertion that just doesn't compare."

My Major Cost Me Time on the Field
"I have been able to study the major of my choice, but it immediately cut my opportunity to play on the field. My coach unfortunately does not view academics as the primary focus, so when I told him I wanted to major in public health, he rolled his eyes and said it would inevitably cost me time on the field (as he pointed to our field). I think that was so wrong because you are penalizing someone for the very reason that they are going to the university. What I find annoying is that when he recruited me (this frustration is reflected upon others in public health) he bragged about the schools top medical program, and the strength of the engineering program, yet once you enter the school, and you tell him that you want to go into medicine or engineering, he actually penalizes you on the field. I find this so contradicting."

Sports Before Internships or Jobs
"I haven't had an internship, and I haven't had a real job. At my first school no one had jobs or internships, because the main focus there was really sports. The coaches would say that academics came first, but it was always the sport and how they would benefit from your athletic performance."

Optimizing University Options
"I was fortunate to be able to take the courses and major that I wanted. I had a leg up because I worked hard in high school. I tested out of some of the courses that we had to take freshman year. I was very adamant on keeping my major. My major was management with an entrepreneurship concentration. I wish that I would've had more time to work in the entrepreneurship center at school and be more entrepreneurial, but I really couldn't with my sport."

No Study Abroad
"We definitely could not study abroad. I tried to go on the business seminars in Korea or Germany. It just wouldn't work. There was one that could've worked if we didn't make the tournament. I couldn't apply for it though, because that would have shown no hope that our team would move onto the tournament. There was another one in the summer that I couldn't do either because of preseason summer training. I think it would've been an awesome experience."

No Internship
"My biggest regret is that I never was able to hold an internship or job because I played football. I like traveling, but I never had time with D1 football. I can't think of any exceptions my coaches have made for any player that would allow someone to spend a semester abroad or off campus, even during off-season in the Spring. You would just miss so much. So no, I never had an opportunity to study abroad. And, not

many people are able to get internships either, unless the internships are really flexible with our football hours. That's another thing I was not able to do because of football. I spent every summer on campus training and practicing."

-- Long Term Tradeoffs --

Friday Travel Will Require an Extra Semester
"I have not been able to take the courses I wanted or needed. I have to be here for another semester. I'll be a semester behind, because the courses I need are offered in the fall, and I would need to be present on Fridays, which never happens with our team travel schedule. So, that's hard."

Longer Program Option
"I am in physical therapy so I could've gone into a program where you finish your undergrad in three years, and then you go to physical therapy school right away your fourth year. You would get accepted right away. I was in soccer, so I couldn't do that. The time wasn't there to do it with soccer, so that was kind of a bummer. Especially now that I'm actually trying to get into PT school. I now realize that it would've been nice to have been able to go straight to PT school my fourth year."

Too Exhausted for Summer Jobs
"My first summer, we had to stay at school for optional yet mandatory practices. It was practice Tuesday and Thursday at 6:45-8:00 am, and then I had summer school afterwards. On top of that we had Monday, Tuesday, Wednesday lifts from 8:30-9:30 am. Doing a summer internship on top of that would've been exhausting, so it wasn't really in the picture. I thought having a job was just so far away, and yet now, the summer before my senior year, I feel very behind and unprepared."

Things to Consider/Check During your Visit:

- Will the coach allow your major?
- Can you have an internship/work experience?
- How do you feel about studying abroad? What is your coach's position?
- Have you met the academic advisor? What is your impression?
- How does the team talk about balancing sports and academics?
- Do you know the rules about athlete study halls? Is this comfortable for you? Will you excel by logging hours and studying in a group setting?
- How does the team describe interactions with professors?
- Do the athletes enjoy their academics?
- Is any current athlete in your major? What is their experience in the major?

For Your Consideration ...

Your thoughts about their stories?
What matches your hopes?
What surprises you?
… What will work for you?

Worksheet: Thinking Through Your Academic Success

Review each of the following questions and jot down your ideas. Thinking through the insights and lessons from the athlete interviews will help you know what to look for in your ideal program match.

Considerations from the Athletes Interviewed	Jot Your Thoughts and Ideas Here
Meeting Schedule Requirements	
• Can you do well in early morning practice and be awake for class?	
• Can you actively participate in night classes after rigorous training during the day?	
• Are you comfortable missing class and making up the work on your own?	
• Will you be able to recover academically from missing many Fridays to travel if needed?	
• Are you comfortable to "over-participate" in class to compensate for athletic conflicts?	
• Will you do EXTRA work, more than other students, to compensate for sports? (*Will you resent that?*)	
Balancing Your Major	
• Do you have a good understanding of what's required for your major?	
• Does your major allow the flexibility for training and competing?	
• Will you need a practicum (e.g., nursing, education, etc.)? Will that fit with training?	
• Have you checked the timing of	

required course offerings? Will you miss them during season?	
- Are you prepared to stay an extra semester or year to meet your requirements? Can you afford the extra tuition and expenses?	
- Do you want to take some of your classes online, even though you are at college on campus?	
Working with Professors	
- Are you ready to build relationships with professors so they can help you navigate your academics?	
- Are you ready to deal with professors who might not value athletics?	
Opting for Unique Learning Opportunities	
- Do you want an internship?	
- Will an internship increase your chance of getting a good job in your field?	
- Is an internship somewhat required in your field (e.g., computer science, business)	
- Do you want to study abroad? Can you make that work?	
Other Ideas:	

Research Input: Consider the Realities of Getting a Job

Unfortunately, but perhaps realistically, a college degree is not the path to employment that it used to be. Most employers are looking for more than a degree, and most graduates find it takes six months, or longer, to find a position. Your participation as an athlete will be an asset in the job search, but you'll need more than that. Here's how to put it in perspective.

The Job Outlook 2016 survey was conducted from August 5, 2015, through September 13, 2015 among the National Association of Colleges and Employers (NACE) employer members. A total of 201 employer members participated in the survey, showing a 20.1% response rate. Based on this report, employers are looking for the following attributes in new job candidates.

Attributes employers seek on a candidate's resume	% of respondents
Leadership	80.1%
Ability to work in a team	78.9%
Communication skills (written)	70.2%
Problem-solving skills	70.2%
Communication skills (verbal)	68.9%
Strong work ethic	68.9%
Initiative	65.8%
Analytical/quantitative skills	62.7%
Flexibility/adaptability	60.9%
Technical skills	59.6%
Interpersonal skills (relates well to others)	58.4%
Computer skills	55.3%
Detail-oriented	52.8%
Organizational ability	48.4%
Friendly/outgoing personality	35.4%
Strategic planning skills	26.7%
Creativity	23.6%
Tactfulness	20.5%
Entrepreneurial skills/risk-taker	18.6%

Source: *Job Outlook 2016*, National Association of Colleges and Employers
http://www.naceweb.org/s11182015/employers-look-for-in-new-hires.aspx

Influence of Attributes	2016 Average Influence Rating*	2015 Average Influence Rating*
Major	4.0	3.9
Has held leadership position	3.9	3.9
Has been involved in extracurricular activities (clubs, sports, student government, etc.)	3.6	3.6
High GPA (3.0 or above)	3.5	3.6
School attended	2.9	2.8
Has done volunteer work	2.8	2.8
Is fluent in a foreign language	2.2	2.4
Has studied abroad	2.0	2.1

*5-point scale, where 1=No influence at all, 2=Not much influence, 3=Somewhat of an influence, 4=Very much influence, and 5=Extreme influence.

Source: *Job Outlook 2016*, National Association of Colleges and Employers
http://www.naceweb.org/s11182015/employers-look-for-in-new-hires.aspx

> *"Challenge is the pathway to engagement and progress in our lives. But not all challenges are created equal. Some challenges make us feel alive, engaged, connected, and fulfilled. Others simply overwhelm us. Knowing the difference as you set bigger and bolder challenges for yourself is critical to your sanity, success and satisfaction."*
>
> -Brendon Burchard, *New York Times Bestselling Author*

6
Plan for Common Challenges

Sitting on the threshold of college athletics, you have done it. You are an experienced athlete. You've come this far, and accomplished great things. You are used to hard work and exhaustion. You are used to winning and losing. You might even be used to the grueling cycle of injury and recovery.

But, almost unanimously, the athletes interviewed for this book described that they were not prepared for the intensity and challenges of D1 college athletics. Their stories are included here to help you greet your move into college athletics with honesty and readiness, so that you can be successful despite the potential hurdles.

Long ago, Benjamin Franklin said, *"By failing to prepare, you are preparing to fail."*

But, you are smarter than that. You will be ready.

Before you read their stories,
- **What challenges worry you?**
- **How will you prepare?**

Stories about the Common Challenges
Insights from D1 athletes about homesickness, travel, mental toughness, injury, etc.

In this section, the stories have been grouped by common themes, to help clarify some of the major considerations in handling the routine challenges that face D1 athletes. The sections included are as follows:

- The Mental Game
- Not Enough Personal Time
- Injuries Happen
- The Unexpected

As throughout the book, the stories remain in the original words of the athletes.

-- The Mental Game --

Worrying About Playing Time
"I worried about playing time. It was a constant worry. With college soccer, you're getting new recruits every single year. If you get complacent at all, you're completely screwing yourself over. New recruits will come in and the coach obviously likes them a lot because he recruited them. They will get the benefit of the doubt more often than not. People are always coming in to take your spot, that's just the name of the game. My entire four years at school I was fighting for playing time. Honestly, I really didn't get the playing time I wanted until my senior year, but I worked my butt off all four years to get it."

Surviving Injury
"I was left behind when my team traveled for a whole season. It was very hard but I 100% grew up and completely changed my perspective. I used the time to catch up in school and study. Plus, my physical therapy was very intense. I had to go twice a day for months. I was sort of preoccupied with that. I have to say that the injury really made me grow up. It turned me into a better student and a better athlete. It changed my perspective completely."

Not Traveling
"I was on a team of 29 girls and my coach only usually traveled 18... even though the school would pay for 22. So there were always like 11 of us left home. Our strength coaches would run us for hours on the days when the team was away. They told us we should be punished for not being good enough, and to run until we got better. They would make us run a timed mile, and then another mile, which we would have to run even faster to beat the previous mile time we earned. That would go on for like 4-5 miles, until girls were puking, could not move anymore, or stopped with injuries. They

would just laugh and tell us to work harder or we would have to see them again the next time the team traveled. We were literally being punished for not being chosen to travel, as if not traveling was not punishment enough. It was miserable."

Proving Yourself AGAIN for New Coaches
"I was personally really tired of getting new coaches and having to prove myself over and over again. So, because of that, I really did not like my new coach. I did not want to talk to him; I just rebelled from whatever he said because in my head I believed that he was going to leave like the rest of my coaches had. And that really affected our relationship. It's hard to have your coach keep leaving you."

Always Feeling Replaceable
"All the time I worry. You come in thinking D1 is your dream, with all the confidence that you will succeed because you have worked so tirelessly to get there. And then you are there, busting your butt, and you overhear your coaches talking about the next group coming in and how they have never seen such talented players. It's hard to not let that get to your head. Its hard always feeling replaceable. And, even harder for my teammates to hear, because many relied on their scholarships to attend."

Mental Focus and Toughness
"I think the mental part is the hardest. Like you have to be mentally in every training session, even if you just had to take a bio test. You have to be mentally tough, because you are really the only one that looks out for yourself. You don't have your parents any more giving their opinion on how a practice or a game went. You have to advocate for yourself, and you have to choose what kind of mentality you want to come with every single day to practice. I thought that the hardest part would be the physical part, but for me it ended up being the mental part."

So Many Ups and Downs
"The most difficult thing is being mentally tough. There are just so many ups and downs. If you get down on yourself, it is very easy to keep going down in a downward slope. You have to figure out how to pick yourself up, especially on things like if you do or don't make the travel squad."

-- Not Enough Personal Time --

Limited Personal Time
"One thing I really didn't like was never having my own time. We were basically like slaves always at the football facility, even eating our meals there daily. It just wears on

you. When you are a freshman you don't mind as much, but even then you are forced into study hall hours, which takes even more time away. The 40-hour in season rule is complete bullshit. We went way over that every week. Every single week."

Always Training
"Academics are very hard. I hardly have time to read a book. On Fridays we have practice from 1:00-5:30pm, and I have no class on Friday, but I never do any school work because I have a lot of extra work I need to do up at the field to become better. I mean over spring break I was up at the field almost every single hour of the day. Literally I could not catch a break, I guess rules don't really apply, so I was there every single hour of every single day."

Your Sport Never Stops
"High school soccer and college soccer are extremely different. In college at Division 1, your sport dictates your every move daily. Your schedule revolves around practice times and team meetings, so that you are basically on a completely different schedule than other college students. In high school, that is not the case. You can be an athlete and still be around your peers all day. You have practice and games after school, but you are still a large part of the school community. In college, athletics separates you, and your identity is strictly athlete. What you don't realize as a high school student picking a D1 college is that you won't be able to go home every night, or go home on weekends to recharge in a space not consumed by sport. You won't see family and friends on a regular basis because D1 never stops."

Not Home for Breaks
"Breaks are tough. Winter break is the hardest because it is the only significant amount of time to be home. We miss about three weeks of that break. It is really challenging. I am going to school in Chicago, but I am from New York, so I don't get to spend time with my family very often. Spring break is only a week long for us, and it's spent traveling to meets. I obviously love competing, but it is sometimes really difficult to stay motivated during a break when you are missing your family."

Little Time at Home
"I didn't have any breaks (chuckle). Like the year I went to Rome for a semester, I counted it out: from January 1st to December 31st, I was home for 13 days. Some of that has to do with making the NCAA's because you don't get spring break when you compete in them. But if you don't make the NCAA's then you do get spring break. But a group of us, including myself, made it every year. So we never had spring break. Winter break was a week and a half at home. I would sometimes go back on the 26th of December to school though. And then fall break, you don't get to do what you want, but you do get to go to Miami for the week and train. So you are training but it is also

really fun. That's a common thing with swim teams. And I think a bunch of other teams."

Missing Classes
"I really wish someone told me I was going to miss so many classes. I am the type of student that is uncomfortable asking someone else for his or her notes, someone I don't know to do my work for me. You'd be lying in a hotel when you were supposed to be in class. That was just a rotten feeling because you would just lie there thinking about how much your parents pay for tuition. That blows."

No Options Besides Sports
"There are definitely people that get really down on themselves. Playing a college sport is very difficult. All D1 sports are a full time job. Don't let anyone tell you otherwise. There is not much of an opportunity to get involved in the rest of campus, or even meet people outside of your classmates and teammates, or other athletes. The time commitment is a big obstacle that takes getting used to. You have to know coming in that besides school and your sport, there is not going to be time for a social life. Even in the off season we workout and train 5 days a week. You get one or two nights off, but that's it on a good week. So, when you choose D1, you are choosing that lifestyle, so it has to be truly what you want to do."

-- Injuries Happen --

Injury Changes Everything
"I tore my labrum in the middle of my sophomore year and it caused me to sit out half of my sophomore season. For me, this really sucked because I was starting, and I was playing, and I had a strong role on my team until I got hurt. I used to play a lot and be at the center of conversations, but then when I got hurt, I started to sit on the end of the bench on game days. My coach made me schedule my rehab during practice, so I was never in practice and didn't really know what was going on. They put new plays in and I would watch the game and wonder what the hell was going on. I just felt segregated from the team. My name was on the roster, but at the same time I felt like a fan, being on the outside looking in. It was really hard for me to have basketball taken away from me."

Concussion
"I had to redshirt my sophomore year because I got a concussion in practice towards the end of the season, right when our conference tournament was about to start. It was on a corner kick, and my teammate and I both went in to clear it away and his knee hit my head. I wasn't able to go to school or do homework for a month. My

trainer was great. He was extra careful making sure I didn't do anything to make my symptoms worse. I just had to sit in my room and stay away from lights. I was finally able to do school work with about a week left of school. All my teachers allowed me to finish the classes except one. By the time I was back the season was over."

Patience to Recover
"I had never been injured before my junior year in college. I was just picking up pace, and then in the second game of the season, a girl fell on top of me and broke my ankle. It was heart breaking. I had just come into preseason in the best shape I had ever been in. It was so tough having my first injury at that age, because I didn't know how to handle it mentally. I was very down on myself. I was worried I wouldn't be back for an entire month, because I didn't know what that would mean. I had to miss four games. It is crazy how much trainers know how to deal with players mentally, because it is as much psychological as it is physical. I had to work with my trainer a lot one-on-one just to handle the thought process of taking everything one minute, one hour, one day at a time. If I kept looking so far in the future like I was, I would've been done mentally. I slowly figured out how to take things day by day through my rehab. There were days that my trainer had to deal with me breaking down and bawling my eyes out. I was just so frustrated, because I didn't know how to make it go faster."

Learning to Take Care of Myself
"I have had several injuries. Not any right now. Knock on wood. I think I've been learning how to take better care of my body from this experience. Freshman year I had bad hips, sophomore year I pulled my quad (it was just overused during preseason) and my spring sophomore year I had a bad ankle sprain. All in all I feel like I've gotten out pretty good compared to a lot of people, so I really can't complain."

You Must Pace Your Recovery
"I came in my freshman year three months post ACL reconstruction, so I got right into doing physical therapy with the athletic staff. That was fine. It was very rigorous. I guess the only thing that I would say is that when I came back from winter break I was pretty much full on. I was playing on hard wood gym floors. I think only once or twice when they let me do an elliptical workout instead of a treadmill workout. So I would just say, that you have to really hold that line where you are comfortable playing, because if you do get hurt again, you are the only one that has to deal with that."

-- The Unexpected --

Non-Injury Redshirt
"I didn't expect to red shirt as a freshman, but I knew in the back of my head that it was definitely a possibility. Size and strength is a big part of your position so having a

year to get stronger, get better, it helped me immensely. I will be a much better player this fifth year then I would have been my freshman year. I look at it as a positive, but that is my outlook. I know a lot of guys who just want to play. But I think it was a good experience because it gave me a year to get acclimated to the campus, to get acclimated to being in college, and have Saturdays that were not super stressful with traveling and stress about going and playing in front of thousands of people. You don't have to worry and stress about messing up on TV. So I'd say it was a positive experience for me that reduced the pressure my first year."

Team Departures
"It's really frustrating when you develop strong relationships with teammates and then they leave at the end of the season. One of my really good friends is transferring and it just sucks because you develop this really strong goofy relationship, and she's one of my best friends on the team, and now she's leaving. It also sucks because she is from around here, and this school has been her dream school since she was a kid, and to see her leave because of our coach is not a nice sight. It's hard to stay when your coach is someone who doesn't relate well to you, and who is constantly barking orders at you, and who creates no sense of community or camaraderie on the team. The only reason I stayed all four years is because of my teammates who have helped me overcome mental blocks and get through hard things. I attribute all my success to them."

Wake Up Call
"Freshman year, in the winter, I fractured my wrist. That was a big wake up call, because all you ever have known is playing your sport. It's very easy to think it'll last forever. I was out for ten weeks, and I wasn't really training. It made me realize that when you're choosing a school you have to make sure that, even if it didn't have your sport, that you would be happy. Personally I feel like I enjoyed my time despite being hurt. It made me feel like I made a good decision to come here."

Missing Friends
"The problem is if you have the academics down and the athletics down, we always forget about the social. We always forget about friendships, and being with people, and having the college experience. Unfortunately, usually when you are doing the school and athletics really well, social does not exist or it's very, very limited. That was my problem freshman year. In my sophomore year I started losing hope in the athletic process. I wasn't making gains, and I wasn't feeling a part of the team. So, I shifted my focus to the academics and to my social life. That definitely diminished how well I did athletically."

For Your Consideration ...

Your thoughts about their stories?
What matches your thoughts?
What surprises you?
… What will work for you?

Worksheet: Preparing for Challenges

Can I handle the potential challenges and still personally win?

It's not fun, but it's necessary to plan for the worst. Reflecting on the experience of these athletes, what strategies can you bring to college to help you best handle the most typical challenges of college athletics?

What if I don't travel or play?
What if I feel undervalued or replaceable?
What if my coach leaves?
What if I'm injured?
What if I can't get home?

What are your other worries about college and athletics?

> *"Begin with the end in mind. Start with the end outcome and work backwards to make your dream possible."*
> -Wayne W. Dyer

7

Informed Recruiting: Finding a Great Match

We started this book from the premise that "beginning with the end in mind" would help you find the college match that would bring fulfilling athletics, academics, and much more. Through the stories of 60 D1 athletes, you have gained an inside perspective about life as an athlete. You've peeked into their routines and challenges, their ups and downs, their bests and worsts. Now, it is time for you to use their lessons to inform your college search and selection – so that you find a place that's right for you. Recruiting is more than just grabbing a D1 spot: it's actually about finding a match that makes you happy, provides great athletics and great academics, and ultimately paves the way for success beyond college.

This section provides insight to help you look beyond the flashy packaging and allure during your recruiting visits, and instead, be alert to the realities that will become the fabric of your life when you join the program.

We believe that you will get an offer... it's picking the right offer that presents the greatest challenge.

This section is about helping you gather practical insights so that you feel prepared to make informed decisions about your life on campus and in the athletic program. As a rising athlete, it's hard to know what you have yet to experience; it's hard to see the reality when you don't know what you're looking for. This book is meant to help you fill the gaps, and remain confident and in control of every opportunity that comes your way.

- Read Between the Lines: There are two sides to everything, and it's important to think through the impacts as you decide where to commit.
- Tools for Recruiting Visits:
  – Athlete Questions During Recruiting
  – Parent Assignments During Recruiting
  – Reflection Log

Your time is now! Good luck!

Read Between the Lines

The college athletic experience is different for everyone. For some, it is the launching pad to education and confidence one never dreamed possible. For others, it is a match gone completely wrong, that creates quite the opposite of physical and mental well-being. Interestingly, because of the guidance and standards of the NCAA, college programs should carry similar features and standards. But sometimes, reading between the lines is the best way to know what's actually going on, and how it will impact an athlete in the program. In other words, there are two sides to every story -- including college athletics.

Academic advisors will help me get the most from my major and course options.

> Yes -- Academic advisors can be a wonderful resource for any college student. They tend to keep a pulse on the academic environment and they develop positive relationships with many professors. They understand the requirements of majors and graduation, and they will help clear hurdles and help you effectively navigate the academic journey from first year transition to graduation.
>
> But,
> Academic advisors for athletes are helping to insure that course requirements can be met around athletic requirements. They work in concert with the coaching staff to insure that the athlete can attend practice and competitions, and also complete the required coursework. In some instances they may recommend courses or professors that are 'sports-friendly,' – the options that make it easier to meet rigorous athletic demands, but might not provide you the best learning and career foundation.

The coach seems to love me. He/she has the players' best interest in mind.

> Yes -- Many coaches become well-loved role models for the athletes in their care. They provide support way beyond the bounds of sport, and help their athletes grow and mature into well-rounded adults who will flourish long after their athletic days. These 'hero' coaches seem to provide 24/7 advice to the students in their care, and help them balance school, sport and social issues, and much more. Athletes who find themselves working with these holistic coaches, who drive toward overall well-being, are indeed, very lucky.
>
> But,
> College coaches are under pressure (and perhaps contract) to win, and winning often requires significantly pushing the current players, or replacing

the current players with even better options. The metrics for success and long-term employment of a college coach may run counter to supporting the individual needs and development of the players. While a coach may want to keep a mid-performance player because they have a strong relationship, the financial realities of limited scholarships, travel budgets, training staff, etc. might make that practically impossible. While a coach might want to develop all the talent on the team, the pressure drives them to focus on those who can play together to win, and to constantly seek new players who can improve the overall team performance. The hope of long-term relationships and loyalty is sometimes at odds with the metrics of the system.

If the coach discusses my role during recruiting, then I'll for sure play for the team.

Yes -- It is great to get a sense of where you fit on a team, and how you can prepare to best fill the spot as needed. It is reinforcing to have a coach discuss the specific opportunity that lies ahead. It is a tremendous win-win if this actually works out.

But,
Coaches are continually, relentlessly looking for talented players and recruiting the best that they can get. The 'who's who' of the team is in constant motion with the goal of winning. There are no guarantees. Let me repeat, there are absolutely no guarantees. A player can be a starter for freshman and sophomore year, and then never see the field again. A player can be recruited with great promise, only to find a new recruit in that position during pre-season. The only thing for sure, is that nothing is for sure in college athletics. Players should love practice as much as competition, because practice is the only guarantee that you get.

If I play my first year, I'm going to play all four years.

Congratulations if you join a D1 team and begin competing as a freshman. That is a tremendous accomplishment, and you should consider it an honor and a privilege. If your skills are good enough to get you out there from the start, they just might be good enough to keep you playing all four years.

But,
A typical D1 coach is frequently contacting high schools and attending tournaments in search of great players. While you may be a star in your position, and he/she is not actively looking to fill your spot, it might happen

that a better recruit surfaces. And, the cycle continues, year after year, with players being replaced as new talent appears. Longevity is most often in service of winning, not loyalty.

If I don't like it, I can transfer and find another school.

Yes -- There are almost 1,900 universities in America with college-level sports. Not every campus has every sport, but it is certain that dedicated, qualified athletes have options to find a spot where they can be happy. In some instances, coaches and staff will use their personal contacts to help players find new programs. This can be a mutually rewarding experience. And for sure, the transfer process requires looking at programs in new ways, so that you don't make the same mistake twice.

But,
There are a few issues that make transferring difficult, but not impossible.

First, a D1 athlete can't leave the school where they committed of their own doing; they need a signed letter of release from their coach. When the athletic situation has become tense, obtaining this release can be emotionally challenging for an athlete, and it is not mandatory for a coach to comply.

Second, an athlete cannot pursue an alternative coach until they have a signed release letter from their existing coach and athletic director. This means that they are often tensely waiting to pursue alternatives, and/or they fall out of normal recruiting cycles when they are finally able to build relationships.

Third, athletes by nature are not quitters, and transferring is often considered to be like quitting. This causes deep personal emotional stress and can flare tense relationships with teammates. So, bottom line, yes it is possible to transfer – but it comes with organizational and personal challenges that will need support.

I competed on winning varsity teams in high school, and for elite clubs. I'm ready for college.

> You Bet! -- The combination of competitive high school athletics and elite club sports is perhaps the best training that you can have for college athletics. If you are adding routine, significant workouts where you constantly push yourself to a new personal best, then you are heading in the right direction. Most likely, with the dream of playing in college, you've taken advantage of the options for personal development that are within reach. If you are physically and mentally ready to keep pushing, then you've done your best to get prepared.
>
> But,
> The physical rigor and demands of college athletics far exceeds most high school and club level programs; the reality is that very few athletes are adequately prepared. College athletes report that the pain and exhaustion from training rarely subside. Instead, they learn to push through it, ignoring their bodies' natural signals for rest and rejuvenation.
>
> Many compare college athletics to a full time job, and even if the hours don't quite match up – the rigor and stress certainly equate.
>
> To be ready, is not a matter of accomplished preparation, but rather the physical and emotional strength to start over at the next level.

My teammates will be my best friends.

> Yes -- Our research shows that 'teaming' is one of the key factors, and probably the brightest hope for incoming college athletes. And for many, this dream becomes a reality and relationships on and off the field are forged so solidly, that they are support beams throughout life. Athletic bonds cemented through sweat and tears run much deeper than other types of friendship. These are like pillars that hold strong for years to come.
>
> But,
> There are a limited number of athletes who will play and travel to play. The 'team' is actually a pool of players competing to gain one of the coveted spots. Add to this the fact that some D1 players have an athletic scholarship that underpins not only their role on the team, but their ability to obtain an education. They must gain playing time, or they risk losing both their sport and their school. Thus, college teams find that players might be working against each other to save themselves individually. The silver lining of ratting out a teammate is that while they sit the bench, you might get in the competition– and get the chance you need to shine and stay.

Add the threat of new recruits to the existing internal competition, and the stress intensifies. The college team can often be the opposite of 'safe and steady' friends.

College peers think that athletes are cool.

Absolutely! -- There is a thrill in getting your new college athletic gear, and strutting in it around campus. There's a halo effect of 'selective toughness' knowing that others know you 'made the cut.' There is an equal thrill when you begin to use the awesome facilities, and think that you have unlimited access to resources that far exceed your previous experience. And there is an honorable humility that grows in knowing that you have joined the legacy of athletes that have played for this amazing organization. Undoubtedly, being a college athlete is very cool.

But,
As time goes on, the shiny new gear becomes a symbol of exhaustion as you wear it for unrelenting practice. And the facilities become routine, and the newness wears away. And when the athletic rigor becomes the new normal, you might realize that college peers have moved on to other things, while you repeat the same demanding cycle. And sometimes your non-athletic friends stop asking you to join, because they assume that you will have practice or a game, like usual. One hard part about athletics is that non-athletes can't get inside the routine, so the social circle of athletes is inherently small. Athletes stick with athletes, and the cool factor for other college peers sometimes wears thin.

For Your Consideration ...

Your thoughts about "two sides to every story"?

Athlete Questions During Recruiting

For the Coaching Staff:
- ☐ What attributes do you look for in athletes?
- ☐ Can you describe your best athletes from the last couple of years? What made them stand out?
- ☐ How many athletes are on the roster?
- ☐ What's the typical training schedule?
- ☐ What's the training like after a game/competition?
- ☐ How many athletes typically play/compete in a game/competition? Do you rotate athletes?
- ☐ How many athletes travel? What is required for those who don't travel?
- ☐ How do we train in the off-season? Summer?
- ☐ What is the scholarship renewal process like? Have you ever taken a scholarship away? Why?
- ☐ Will I be allowed to go home for holidays?
- ☐ Are there any majors that athletes can't take due to athletic requirements?
- ☐ How many classes did your athletes miss last season due to competition and travel?
- ☐ Can I do an internship?
- ☐ Can I study abroad?
- ☐ Do you see yourself staying at this institution for the next four years?

For the Athletic Training Staff:
- ☐ How do you typically work with the non-injured athletes? Do you facilitate any injury prevention?
- ☐ How many athletes are usually injured in a typical season?
- ☐ What are the common injuries you see? How are they handled?
- ☐ How does the (name of sport) Coach treat athletes who are injured?

- ☐ Do you attend all practices and games?
- ☐ How many teams do you work with?

For the Current Athletes: *(Crucial to take an overnight visit, or two ...)*
- ☐ How do you like this university?
- ☐ Do you like your coach?
- ☐ How would you describe him/her?
- ☐ What is his/her coaching style like in practice and games?
- ☐ Do you feel well cared for and respected as an athlete here?
- ☐ Do you ever feel pushed too hard? Over-trained? Exhausted?
- ☐ Were any athletes injured last year? Do the athletic trainers provide good treatment? How does you coach respond to injuries?
- ☐ How did your freshman year go? Did you get to play?
- ☐ Do you have friends outside of your team?
- ☐ Are you involved in any campus clubs/activities outside of your sport? Does your coach support this?
- ☐ Have you held an internship or studied abroad? Can you?
- ☐ Were you able to pick your major and attend class regularly? How are your academic advisors?
- ☐ Can you go home for holidays and/or the summer?
- ☐ How many people have transferred/quit this program while you have been here? Why?
- ☐ What's the worst part of being an athlete here?
- ☐ If you could start all over, would you pick this school, this athletic program?

Parent Assignments During Recruiting

- ☐ **Learn from other parents:** Get in touch with other team parents and ask questions. It is important to talk to parents of sophomore players, because their memories of the transition year are still most vivid.

    - How hard was it to get started with the team?
    - Was the coach supportive?
    - Were the other athletes inclusive of the freshman?
    - Was there any hazing? (Yes, this is still a possibility...)
    - What tips do you have to ease the transition?

- ☐ **Hang around and ask the current athletes questions:** The current athletes hold invaluable knowledge. They have experience of all aspects of both student life, and life as an athlete. Take advantage of what they know by asking them questions about their current experience. Of course, be mindful of both the right time and place for truthful responses (not around coaching staff or athletic personnel). Their words paint a true picture of life as a student-athlete.

    "Actually, when the parents ask the players, it is even more beneficial, because we're 100% honest with them. Parents should really play a bigger part in asking good questions. I think it's important to ask about what the environment is like, how the girls are, and what relationships with the coaches are like. "   - Athlete Interview

- ☐ **Questions for Current Players**

    - What is the team environment like? Supportive? Competitive?
    - Do you have a good relationship with your coach?
    - Has your coach gotten to know you as more than just an athlete?
    - Do you have good relationships with your teammates? The older athletes?
    - Do you enjoy going to practice?
    - Do you feel well cared for by trainers and coaches?
    - How much playing time do freshmen usually get? Do they travel?

- Does your coach set academics as first priority?
- What is the hardest part about being an athlete here? What do you wish was different?

☐ **Hang around and ask other students questions:** It is invaluable to take advantage of the spontaneous, unguarded conversations that you can have while hanging around the campus. It is important to ask anyone who will talk to you for observations about athletics in general, and your team in particular.

- How are the athletes on campus? Do students attend athletic events?
- Do athletes mix in clubs/Greek life beyond athletics?
- Do you know anything about the (name of sport) team?
- Have you heard anything about Coach _____?
- Do you have any friends that are athletes? What do they tell you about life as an athlete here?

☐ **Learn informally from the athletic trainer:** Try to meet, individually and informally, with the trainer assigned to the team/sport. Build a rapport to suggest that you need their honest guidance in making this important decision. Let him/her know that your child's health is your biggest priority, and you need their input and expertise.

- How many athletes on the team are currently injured? Is this typical?
- What are the common things you treat?
- Is there a tendency for overtraining?
- Is there sufficient time for normal rest and recovery?
- Are players allowed to fully recover from injury without pressure?
- Is there medical support available at all games/meets? At practices?
- What medical facilities are used in case of emergency?

Make copies of this page to use on each campus visit

Reflection Log

College: _____

Date of Visit: _____

Meeting With: _____

Initial Thoughts & Reactions Post Visit:
(Brief words, descriptions, recollections that paint a lasting picture of your visit for you to refer back to.)

- *The coach made me feel….*
- *The other athletes made me feel…*
- *Being on campus made me feel…*
- *The athletic facilities …*

What I learned about the **athletic** program:

What I learned about the **academic** programs:

One thing that caught my attention:

Overall, three positives of this college:
-
-
-

Overall, three negatives of this college:
-
-
-

Can I see myself spending four years here?

Additional questions/concerns I need to pursue:

More Notes on this College Visit ---
   What about the coach?
   What about the team?
   What did you like the most?
   What worries you?
   … What will work for you?

Appendices

Appendix 1: Research Summary

Two Division 1 athletes were recruited to conduct the 60 interviews included in this book. The researchers took a qualitative approach to this study, in order to gather real life stories of experiences within NCAA D1 athletics. Qualitative research is a common research design that allows for rich, detailed understanding of a real life phenomenon; in this case, life as a D1 college athlete. The researchers used their personal background in sport to recruit D1 athlete participants (initially via email) who were willing to volunteer to take part in this effort to gather and share an inside peek of college athletics. Before commencing athlete interviews, researchers were trained in qualitative research collection, and a research guide including detailed semi-structured interview questions, was developed (to be precisely followed by both researchers) in an effort to ensure consistent and accurate data collection. Verbal consent to use athlete stories in this book was gained from each athlete before beginning interviews. Additionally, with athlete permission, all interviews were audio recorded in order to ensure accurate transcription of individual's personal words post interview during the transcription process. Each interview lasted approximately 40 minutes in length. Both researchers participated in transcribing the interviews verbatim (*in exactly the athlete's words*), and all interviews were checked a final time for accuracy by the first researcher. Overall, researchers spoke with 60 D1 athletes and coded nearly 1,000 stories from their interviews.

Remember: The book is a compilation of individual stories. **It is not an analysis of the sports, the teams, or the programs included**. The stories are provided with the sole goal of providing real-life insight on life as a D1 athlete by illuminating potential benefits and demands of the D1 lifestyle.

Research Statistics

    60 Interviews: 65% female; 35% male

    Sports Included (Both men's and women's when appropriate)

Baseball	Soccer
Basketball	Swimming
Cross Country	Tennis
Equestrian	Track and Field
Football	Volleyball
Golf	
Lacrosse	

University and College Programs Included

Ball State	Nebraska
Butler	Northwestern
Cleveland State	Northern Illinois
Columbia	Ohio State
Creighton	Princeton
Dartmouth	Purdue
DePaul	Saint Joseph
Duke	Saint Louis University
Eastern Michigan	Santa Clara
Elon	Southern Methodist University
Indiana University	University of Cincinnati
Georgia Southern	University of Kentucky
John Hopkins	University of Minnesota-Twin Cities
Louisiana Tech	University of Tennessee, Chattanooga
Louisville	Wofford College
Loyola Chicago	Xavier
Manhattan	

Appendix 2: The Research Approach

Below is the interview guide used by the research team conducting athlete interviews.

Athlete Interview Guide (as of January, 2016)
RESEARCH PROTOCOL

1. Introduce yourself (name/background) and the study (use the format below)

PROJECT: This project is a national research effort to gather and share an inside peek of college athletics with families who are currently facing the D1 decision. Each interview should be around 40 minutes.

GOAL: Our goal is to collect 100+ interviews translating to 1000+ stories across the landscape of D1 college athletics.

Below are key points you should mention when interviewing an athlete. It is important to provide them with background information on the *purpose* of the interview, and why we are gathering these interviews. Also remind them of our *confidentiality promise*.
- "To play or not to play?" — a question facing many high school athletes and parents across the country.
- As early as sophomore year in high school, students are personally wondering or perhaps being actively recruited to play college sports.
- This decision has significant academic, financial, social, and long-term personal ramifications.
- We are conducting interviews across the nation to gain feedback on current student athletes and their experiences—in an effort to educate future generations of athletes.

OUR MISSION: May the book from this project provide a useful context to help these families make an informed college athletic decision.

OUR PROMISE: All identifying information will be held as strictly confidential. The final publication may only reference:
- Gender of interviewee
- Sport Played
- Name of school (only in an appendix; never tied directly to a story)
- Size of school
- Region school is located in (ex: Midwest)

All names (personal and school) and any other identifying information will be removed from specific stories prior to adding content to the book. Athlete identity will remain strictly confidential.

2. ***After describing the above, ask for their verbal consent to use the stories they share in a future book (only continue if consent is gained)***

3. ***Ask permission to record the interview via "call recorder app" (begin recording only if athlete verbally consents)***

4. ***With consent to interview, and consent to record, you may now begin your interview following the 'interview guide' below:***

General Research Questions: Please ask interviewee to share as many stories as come to mind for each question. Please ask all questions (including the bullet points) and record detailed answers.

* It is imperative that you record as much information (and in their words) as possible to make a substantial contribution to the book.

1. What are your best memories/experiences of your Division 1 athletic experience?
    - Describe your relationship with your teammates. Is there a great memory you will never forget?
    - Describe your relationship with your coach. What is one great moment you have had with your coach?
    - Do you often do team bonding outside of your sport? Any stories?
    - Overall BEST memory (award, game, practice, big win etc.)?

2. What is the normal routine as a Division 1 athlete? (Please discuss both academics and training, both in-season and off-season)
    - What is your in season routine like (sport & class)
    - What is your out of season routine like (sport & class)
    - Have you been able to take the courses/ major you wanted?
    - How have professors treated you as an athlete?
    - Do you have an academic advisor? Explain relationship.
    - Do you like your athletic trainers/ feel supported?

3. What are your worst memories/experiences of your Division 1 athletic experience?
    - Did you ever have a bad experience with a teammate?
    - Did you ever have a bad experience with a coach?
    - Were you immediately included by your teammates?
    - What are some preseason difficulties?

- What are some academic difficulties?
- How often do you worry about playing time/ a new recruit taking your position?
- Have you ever been left behind when your team travels? How did you feel?
- Any injuries?

4. If you could change certain things about your team/coach/program, what would you do?
   - Do you get regular feedback from your coach?

5. What are the differences between high school athletics and college sport requirements?
   - Differences in school/sport balance
   - What is your social life like outside of your team and sport?

6. What advice would you give to athletes or families making the D1 college choice?
   - If you could go back, would you do anything differently?
   - What is one thing you wish someone told you before you choose your school?

7. Has playing your sport bettered you as a person (not asking about athletics)?

5. Please remember to thank your interviewee! Their stories and insights will be very helpful to the next generation of college athletes.

Appendix 3: Share Your Experiences

We are interested in learning about your experiences in recruiting, transitioning, and living as a D1 athlete, to continue helping upcoming recruits.

About this Book
- What was most helpful?
- What additional information from athletes would have helped you during recruiting?
- What improvements would you recommend?

About Your Recruiting
- How did you learn the "inside scoop" about your potential coach and team?
- What was the most challenging aspect of the recruiting process?
- What was the most surprising thing about the recruiting process?

About Your Transition
- What was most unexpected in transitioning to college athletics?
- What could have made the transition easier?
- How long did it take until you felt comfortable with your team?
- What advice would you give to your former teammates who will make the transition to college athletics?

About Your Life as a College Athlete
- How do you balance athletics, academics and social?
- How do you keep your wellness in the midst of the extreme training/competition?
- How do you maintain confidence when you're not playing?
- How do you keep strong relationships with your teammates?
- How do you build a positive connection with your coach?
- What advice would you give to an incoming player?

Please email all information to **d1dream.info@gmail.com**

Marita Decker

Marita is an international consultant in leadership development, and a personal executive coach. She has worked in various industry and university settings to help frame the competencies and processes that bring out the best in people and organizations. Her interest in athletics was spurred by her three children who are dedicated athletes. Their experiences led her to believe that athletes embody an exceptional capacity for personal leadership, coupled with unrelenting tenacity. Their college environments should be a match which fosters their love of sport, overall health, and holistic success.

Caroline Zadina

Caroline competed at both the D1 and D3 level during her colligate soccer career. As a senior at DePauw University, Caroline achieved university recognition as the top senior female student athlete, NCAC conference recognition, an NCAA playoff appearance, and a nomination for NCAA female athlete of the year. Following college, Caroline continued her competitive soccer career with a semi-professional team in northern England, while completing her Masters in Sport Psychology with Leeds Beckett University. She currently coaches college soccer while pursuing her graduate degree as a clinical psychologist. She is dedicated to helping individuals, especially athletes, achieve their physical and mental best.

Made in the USA
Las Vegas, NV
19 December 2022